The Earl of Lee Heights

Shirley F.B Carter

Goose River Press
Waldoboro, Maine

Copyright © 2021 Shirley F.B Carter

All rights reserved. No part of this book may be reproduced in any form without written permission from the publisher, except by a reviewer who may quote brief passages in a review to be printed in a newspaper or magazine.

Library of Congress Card Number: 2021937416
ISBN: 978-1-59713-234-3

First Printing, 2021

Cover design by Kira Bedoin.

Published by
Goose River Press
3400 Friendship Road
Waldoboro ME 04572
e-mail: gooseriverpress@gmail.com
www.gooseriverpress.com

Dedication

To my multigenerational family members, friends and age mates, especially those of us born in the nineteen-twenties and thirties. Our lives are shaped by our times. I feel connected to all who played outdoors all day, felt safe in our neighborhoods, enjoyed woodlands and farms within the city limits. We can remember walking to our neighborhood school, enjoying an hour for lunch at home and then returning to school for the afternoon. These are memories I want to share. There are few young people who enjoy such treasures now. I am thankful to those who read this memoir and invite you to follow me down memory lane.

Contents

Author's Note   v
Introduction   vi

Water: The Liberator   1
Thirsty: My Journey to Drink It All In   3
Herbert and Dorothy's Daughters   7
Looking Like Topsie   18
Lee Heights   21
Earl of Lee Heights   24
All Things Bright and Beautiful   31
Ten-Yard Roller   37
Love Letters   45
Sparrow   52
Stellar Events   57
Courtroom   61
Friends and Neighbors   69
The Sisterhood   74
Eliane Remax Nagle Landry Harrison   80
Daytona Beach   86
Inés   91
Jogging, Junkets & Just Plain Fun   94
Deep Water Harbor   99
The Beginning   107
Marie, aka Mimi   110
The Ceremony   115
Saying Goodbye   118

Index of Photographs   123

Author's Note

When I was very young and began to wonder about the world, I tried to answer the question, "Who are you?" My early answer was, "I am a child of God." When asked my name, I gave the factual answer: "Barrow." I knew where I came from, the house I lived in and who I belonged to. I did not answer, "Shirley." My first name did not seem to belong to anyone else, but a stranger who did not accept my Sunday School answer would know who I was if I answered "Barrow." I carried my family with me: living proof of my identity.

Years can be spent trying to know who one really is, beyond the dictates of family and society. Many years of experiences with neighbors, friends and workmates reveal a self that was not so recognizable in youth. The author invites the reader to share her journey and perhaps compare and consider their own quest for identity.

As a young one, the author chose to consider herself an Earl. This identity originated from her mother's playful naming of their humble home as "Lee Heights." Mother and daughter were both trying to lift their spirits from the harsh reality of an unfinished, poorly heated shelter with no running water or electricity. Events in the story take place from the nineteen-thirties up to the present day. Life stories are always unique, and when shared, even with family members raised in the same household in the same era, one can discover savory surprises and hidden connections. *The Earl of Lee Heights* is an invitation to the reader to explore the life of a New England colored girl. May you be inspired as well to share your own story.

Introduction

Herbert Hoover was president when my family was living on Putnam Avenue in Cambridge, Massachusetts. I was born "over the bridge," as my mother would say, in Boston. As the Great Depression worsened, my father put the household furnishings in storage and took his wife and two daughters to his sister's house several towns away, in Sharon. My sister, Audrey, and I were young, about ages two and three.

I was already curious about my identity. The brief stay in Sharon made it clear we were not part of the Drummond family. My father didn't stay there with us. Sharon was freezing that winter, and our reception there was equally cold.

My mother's parents gave my father and mother a gift of land on Ellen Street in Worcester, MA. Our home was to be built there. My father left us well before the house was constructed; there was only tar paper on the outside, and no windows upstairs. Growing up in Worcester kept me searching for identity and wondering. Classism and racism made it very clear that we were different. I began my schooling at Roosevelt Elementary. It was walking (often running) distance from my house. My maternal grandfather, Elias E. Rickards, was the school janitor. He was called "Jan." Some of the older boys befriended him due to their common interest in homing pigeons. Grampa was an expert at raising and showing exotic birds, chickens and rabbits: Mendelian breeder, predictor of pelt and color, and robber of my grandmother's garden carrots!

For twenty-one years, I remained a Worcester resident: attending Grafton Street Junior High, Classical High School (college prep) and later, as a working mother, the St. Augustan Institute of Assumption College, completing my BA and MA at Assumption College. At that time, Assumption College was only for men, and the prep school curriculum was taught in French.

It was at City Hospital where I was not alone in my concern about my identity. The Worcester City Council knew my sister and I were of African heritage, and when we applied to enter the Worcester City Hospital School of Nursing, it became a "problem." When supportive educators learned of the difficulty, we were advised to identify ourselves as Portuguese on our applications. No way. At that time, I identified as Colored.[1] I was seventeen. We persevered, endured and, after a remarkable process, we were admitted. The prestigious co-ed nursing school established in 1871 trained nursing leaders known world-wide. In 1949, our basic sciences were taught at Worcester State College, and the credits were valid at other colleges. This was very advanced for the times.

Oh, the places I went after graduating from Worcester City Hospital School of Nursing in 1952! Right after graduation (and the ensuing celebration), I lived in Germany for six months. An American Express Tour took us, me and my sister, to Paris and to Rome. We toured Bavaria, dined in Baumholder on the French border and, as dependents of a field grade officer, crossed the Atlantic twice on troop transport ships.

On returning stateside in 1953, I spent two thirty-day stints being observed in two institutions: one private in Brattleboro, Vermont, and the other in Taunton State Hospital near Cape Cod. Expressions of rage, stuffed down for years in response to irrational racism and poverty, had exploded. Electroshock treatments and skillful psychological counselling quelled them, and I returned to Worcester to pass my nursing board exams and accept a position as a church camp nurse. Instead, an emergency call for all professional nurses rang out in Worcester.

[1] My memoir, *Colored, of Course* [Goose River Press, 2017], expands on this incident.

Author in Uniform

A tornado had ripped through schools, homes and a housing development. On June ninth, in 84 minutes, 94 people died, and 15,000 were left homeless! I volunteered and was assigned to the old Winslow Surgery, which was the temporary morgue. We, the volunteers and medical staff, worked day and night without stopping. I was hired by Worcester City Hospital, and I remained there for a good five years.

My quest to earn a degree in nursing and a budding romance with Oscar Carter took me to Washington D.C., where I stayed for a short time at my father's house and then moved into my first apartment at 2727 P Street in Georgetown. The advertised nursing "Learn and Earn" program at the Georgetown University Hospital guaranteed a BA in nursing. Duty hours were coordinated with Catholic University classes. I had a federal grant that would cover any tuition costs. I was hired without realizing I was a "first": the first and only Black professional nurse to work there. Roadblock: While setting up my nursing assignment (on the maternity floor) and coordinating my school hours, my supervisor gave me the bad news. The Catholic University did not accept Black students. My dreams were dashed, never to be fulfilled. I worked at the hospital, fell completely in love, eloped and had my first child at Georgetown University Hospital.

Oscar's first job after his graduation was at the Pownal Training School in Maine. Off we went: mama R.N., papa psychologist, and brand-new baby, Laurie. During the winter of 1957, we lived briefly at the school and then in an apartment in Portland overlooking the bay. I worked part-time at the Maine Medical Center. Oscar commuted to Pownal until he found an apartment in Yarmouth, nearer his job. I commuted to the Medical Center until the summer of 1959.

I came home from Portland one day to find that my husband had resigned from his job and emptied our apartment with the aid of boys from the school. I was stunned. We all piled into the car, and the baby and I were summarily dropped off in Worcester at my mother's house.

Newly pregnant, I went to work at Worcester City Hospital. I had come full circle. My life was upside down, and I found myself brazenly sued for desertion.

Who was I now? No longer Mrs. Oscar D. Carter. I was mother, unhappy daughter, fortunate sister, aunt, granddaughter and professional RN. In the years ahead, I added "student" to my list of roles and placed heightened value on my family and friends. They sustained me through the turbulence.

My nursing supervisor encouraged me to answer a call to teach health education in the Worcester Public Schools. Working with healthy, vibrant, beautiful eighth-grade students was a priceless adventure. Those wonderous years when a child is neither hay nor grass, baby nor adult are energy-packed years of discovery. Exhausted and poorly paid, I became a respected teacher, worked in staff development and earned my doctorate in Education from the University of Massachusetts at Amherst. When my course was no longer offered to eighth graders, I taught health educators at Springfield College.

I had been a perpetual teacher; now I became a perpetual student. As an elder, I have taken many free courses at Worcester State College, now Worcester State University. Along with many enjoyable electives, I have sung with the chorus in Professor Nigro's classes for over twenty years. Every two years, the acapella chorale that she trains and teaches travels and performs internationally. For amazing group rates, she invites her chorus students, faculty and parents to accompany the performers. Expanding my love of travel that began in the early 1950s, I have toured Spain, Ireland, Argentina, Portugal, Greece, Sicily, Poland, the Czech Republic, Scotland and Northern Ireland with this group. My very first flight out of the country was to Bermuda to visit my paternal grandfather. I travelled and sang with the College of the Holy Cross across Italy, performing at the Vatican for the Pope. My sister and I have travelled with St. Vincent Hospital employees across the United States, visiting the national parks and taking a Southern grand tour. Audrey's travel club included Broadway shows and allowed us to travel to Switzerland, England, Scotland, Wales, Australia and New Zealand.

My DNA says I am a descendant of the Ticar people, who

originated in what is now known as Cameroon. I know who I am: a worthwhile person who is pleased to share her identity quest and adventures with you. I am an adventurous, curious, sometimes rambunctious, beautiful Black woman.

Also by Shirley F. B. Carter

Colored, of Course

The Roan

CHAPTER 1

Water: The Liberator

This memoir flows from childhood fantasies through a stream of journal entries bringing the reader along the author's river-ride called life. As I glided along, it became clear to me that water is necessary not only to sustain life: in my family history, it has been crucial. Madagascar, Bermuda, the West Indies – all places surrounded by water, impacted by imperialism and colonialism: these are the places from whence my family came. They crossed the waters to America. My paternal grandfather was a ship's carpenter. My maternal great-grandfather escaped slavery by running away and shipping out to England. Ships carrying slaves lost cargo as some chose freedom by leaping overboard to a watery grave. My ancestors and many others like them found water a way of life: fishing and working as "Black Jacks." That's what sailors of color were called in the old times.

Taking a boat to Canada was a path of freedom for my great-grandmother and her husband. The next generation continued going to sea, earning a living by fishing. Women lugged many buckets of water doing laundry. My Aunt Carrie had an outdoor platform where she took in laundry for many of her Cape Cod neighbors, including the large Kennedy family that lived nearby in

Hyannis Port. She remarked that the Kennedy clothes were the dirtiest of all, evidence that those children played rough outdoor games.

Women hauled buckets of water from wells, rain barrels and pumps that needed to be primed. I was fascinated by the large handle pumping motion, the dribble of water needed to chortle up a new gush when Aunt Carrie would rachet (pump) the handle. Watching her was mesmerizing. She was a beautiful woman with wavy, silver grey hair and freckles all over her face and arms. She lost weight as she aged, leaving amazing flaps of loose flesh where her triceps used to be. They flapped like wings, and I wanted arms just like hers.

Water in all forms has majesty. We can walk on water in frigid times and float on its buoyancy at the beach. Both heat and cold mingle to make mist that forms clouds. The major component of our physical being is composed of water: rushing, surging, sparkling, rivers, streams, arteries, veins, sweat and tears, all vital to the history of my people and my very existence. From the Big Continent (Africa) to the small amniotic sac, we are people of water, cradled, buffeted and expelled into a wide universe where all manner of things befall us.

CHAPTER 2

Thirsty: My Journey to Drink It All In

*The greater part of our happiness or misery depends
on our disposition and not our circumstances.*"
—Martha Washington

I was so young, and sometimes I was hungry and
thirsty. Dorothy, my mom, used magic thinking to
chase away those feelings. At night, it was the black
velvet sky dotted with sparkling, winking stars. Magic
Mom could tell stories about their shapes from the
Greek mythology she had learned in grade school.

"See, there's the Big Dipper." At first, as a wee one,
I could not see it. My sister, almost a year older,
encouraged me to keep trying.

"Oh, it's tipping down. I see it!" There was Orion and
the North Star, and we had no trouble finding the Milky
Way.

Even when it was winter, when the family was cold,
hungry and thirsty, the night sky enchanted us and
our mother. The sky rippled. Sheets of shimmering, ici-
cle-like threads pointing down near the horizon flashed
across the sky.

"Ma, the ripples are dancing. What is that?"

Ma smiled. The pleasure in her expression washed
away the effects of the cold and the hunger and the

thirst.

"It's the aurora borealis. Sometimes you will see them in color!"

My mother pointed out constellations and knew their names. Streetlights were absent or dim, so the night sky was a black velvet canopy filled with shimmering celestial bodies. Evenings, we would chant, "Star light, star bright, first star I've seen tonight, I wish I may, I wish I might, have the wish I wish tonight."

Sky watching was exciting and full of pleasure. The moon in all its phases was sheer beauty whether in twilight or at midnight. We were enchanted by rainbows during showers. We gawked at clouds as they floated by. Their changing shapes sparked imagination: herds of sheep, giant fuzzy airplanes and angel hair. They reflected the colors of the rising and setting sun, turned in moments from purple to black, blood red to pink.

My childhood was sandwiched between the physical and social challenges of poverty and racism alongside the wondrous, beautiful natural world. Parents and guardians are responsible for providing food, clothing and shelter for their children. My family and many others struggled to provide basic needs in the late 1920's and 1930's.

In spring and summer, Magic Mom used the woodlands to ward off those familiar feelings of hunger and thirst. We would carry tins of water from Mark Hays' pond and often searched for berries.

"Who can spot the first lady slipper?" All eyes scoured the meadow floor, searching for the orchid-like bloom that stood between two bunny-shaped tall green leaves. Our eyes drank in sprouting vegetation: the curly stems of shiny furry fiddle ferns, every mushroom

and the elusive broad shiny-leafed checkerberry.
Spring brought sprouts of shrubbery across Mark
Hays' pasture. Then I would see it: the pink wild orchid.

Early 12 Ellen Street #1

"Here's one!" We would leave them where they grew
and expected to find more near the pond.

My cousins on both sides of my family lived in the
city. The Boston cousins went to summer camp, so they
were lucky to see velvet night skies and perhaps rainbows, but my Worcester cousins came out to the country when they visited our grandparents, who lived next
to me. It was a treat for them, and they envied us country cousins.

I grew up knowing one could satisfy hunger and
thirst by drinking in the wonders of the universe.

It was at my dying father's bedside that I heard what

guided him through his complicated, sometimes indulgent life. I was three when he abandoned his second wife, my mom, and his two "spring" children. It was his fourth wife and her children with me at the bedside. The Colonel's battle with colon cancer was over. He smiled as his eyes closed for the last time and uttered his advice: "Drink all the wine..."

My life was markedly different from his.

CHAPTER 3

Herbert and Dorothy's Daughters

The cellar is cool and full of odd stuff. I look up at the huge blade hanging in front of my face. I think it's called a scythe: a short handle on a long pole, with that cutting blade on the bottom. Tall people can swing it and cut bushes. The pile of lumber is up to the window. Right inside the door you can see the big black oil barrel. If there is no kerosene in it, I can tell: just bang on it. If it sounds like a big drum with a deep voice, yup, we have oil today. When it is empty, the noise is high pitched, real hollow like a little tin drum, almost like an echo. At the very back of the cellar, there is a long rock ledge. It slants, so you have to be careful getting across to the far side. I can't remember what's over there, and I want to find out. But I hear Ma, and I panic.

She yells. "Shirley, Shirley!"

Oh, oh, I'm going to get it. I go up as slowly as I can.

*"I should have known better than send **you**! What were you doing down there?" She's mad. There's no way to explain how interesting the cellar is and how I forgot why she sent me down there and that I was just about to discover the other side of the ledge.*

"Audrey! Go down there and get me that chair I fixed."

My sister is considered reliable. She's only eleven

months older than me. Ma never calls her names. She just makes her do a lot of stuff, like sewing and embroidering and errands. Ma calls me "Topsie," and I know that's not a good thing. It means my hair is a mess, or there's dirt on my clothes, or I'm just plain stupid. I don't get the switch this time, but I know before the day is over, I'll be called more names. Topsie is some ugly black girl in a book about slaves: <u>Uncle Tom's Cabin</u>. I have never read the book, but I know she must be stupid, dirty and ugly like me. I figure I will just slow down, keep out of sight, take deep breaths and try to forget about getting a whipping. Even then, Ma might still call me by another name if she wants me to do something.

"Stepin Fetchit, get in here and fold these clothes!" Now I've seen Stepin Fetchit in the movies. He is a big old black minstrel guy, with bug eyes and big lips, long droopy arms and shuffling feet. I know I don't look like him, but she is being mean and telling me I move too slow and am stupid!

I hated being called names. At home, it always made me panicky and forgetful. When I slowed down, I was just trying to be cautious and avoid mistakes. It didn't help. As for Audrey, she was stuck being "reliable" for the rest of her life. Ma called on her for anything she herself found challenging. Audrey did all of her errands and served as her executor at death.

The names kids called me at school were familiar taunts. I was never confused about what they meant, nor did I think they believed I was Sambo or a Gold Dust Twin or Jemima. At home, however, it felt as though Ma must be right. I was not relied upon, like my sister. Feeling stupid stuck to me. It seemed I only proved it when I couldn't remember something. Ma was really mad when I was too slow or forgot things. She'd swat me.

But I never stayed mad at her. She was Mama Pig, who protected us from the Big Bad Wolf. The Big Bad Wolf was Dad. He'd left us in the big unfinished house on the hill. It was just a field away from my grandparents, who had given the land to my parents when we left Sharon. Mama Pig kept us warm and could make meals out of nothing. When there was no food in the house, she'd say we were having wind pudding and air sauce for supper. She would find food for us in the woods owned by a neighbor, Mark Hays.

"Here's a sassafras tree. You can eat as many leaves as you like." She'd snap twigs off the black birch trees and let us chew the bark. It tasted like spearmint.

"Look under that tree near the roots where the leaves are piled up. That's where you'll find checkerberries."

I ate mud pies my sister made and decorated with dandelion blossoms. The dandelions were bitter and the pie gritty and it made my sister laugh, because when I made them, she only make-believe ate them. Make-believe was something we thrived on. Ma used to entertain herself and us, too. The three of us made the half-built house our home. Ma called it Lee Heights. Imagination was a life saver for me. It was not as easy for Audrey to turn to her imagination. She was Dorothy's reliable daughter.

I asked Ma one day, "Who am I named after?"

"Well, no one, really." There was a long pause. "Your father's family didn't like the name I chose for you, Robin, but everyone liked the name Shirley."

"Does a whole family choose a name?" I wondered.

"That's the way we did it when you were babies."

My sister was named after my father's maternal aunt, Lizzy: Audrey Elizabeth. We met Aunt Lizzy. She was one ugly, scary woman. Why would anybody name a baby after a wizened, skinny, scowling dark lady who put white powder on her face? We knew another girl named Audrey, but she was the daughter of one of the women chasing after my father. I didn't ask Ma where the name Audrey came from. The only Shirley I knew was that beautiful little girl with the curls who was in the movies: Shirley Temple. She could sing and dance and was very beautiful.

"Ma, you named me after her, didn't you?" I was certain, but Ma always denied it. Maybe that's what Ma hoped for me, but everything around me, from her mean names to the kids at school, made me feel more like the Gold Dust Twins. That red box of soap had two very black children on the front, and they looked like boys to me. Maybe the other kids called us that because my sister and I were the same age for one month every year, and some people thought we were twins.

When I was very little, I remember sitting in a big wicker pram that had a drop down part for the feet. It wasn't a baby carriage. Family would visit, grin in my face and ask me what my name was. Did *they* think I was stupid? They were my relatives. They knew who I was! I'd get so angry and just say, "Barrow." I was a lot older when I discovered my mother put them up to it, just to hear and see a little person get so annoyed.

Church helped me find an imaginary family. It was my secret armor, knowing that God was my father and Jesus my brother. No one knew I had adopted them. It was my secret power. Church also gave me an answer to that awkward question, "And *who* are *you*?" that implied I didn't belong and was out of place. I could proudly answer, "I am a child of God," and the stupid questions stopped. With my secret family, I could withstand anything: name calling, whippings, cold and hunger, all of it.

Before Dad left for good, he was always away somewhere doing Army stuff; my sister and I were known as "Captain Barrow's girls." On his last day with us, he had been at work all day, doing whatever it was he did. Ma had taken us to Mark Hays' woods to find safe berries and leaves to eat. He often became angry when he heard we were foraging. When he came home that day, I cautioned my mom, "Don't tell him we went to the woods." She smiled at me and assured me it would not be a problem. Maybe, like me, she was anticipating he'd be bringing food from Teddie's Market down on Grafton Street. He often brought rice, which I especially like, even today.

When he asked what we had done all day, as if he were genuinely interested, Ma told him that we had been out walking in the woods. She didn't even mention that we had been looking for something to eat, but he was furious.

He raised his voice. "Taking my children into the woods!" He continued to yell about how dangerous it was. I thought, "oh, oh, I told her not to tell him!" Then he reared back and socked her in the face! In my memory, my sister was crying and screaming, but I'm sure I was crying, too. I think he left food for us before he stormed off.

He didn't live with us anymore after that, but he did

drive up one time later. My sister and I were scared. We all went outside. It was as if Ma didn't want him in the house ever again. They argued about something, and Audrey and I just stood there with her in the yard. Ma had planted some flowers beside the path that led to the road. The flowers were small and trimmed with small rocks.

The next thing we knew, he was yelling at her at the top of his lungs, and then he swung his fist, knocking her face down onto the flowers and rocks. She didn't move. I stared at her unmoving body. I was certain he'd killed her, and I dove after his legs, biting down as hard as I could. It was Ma who grabbed hold of me as my father tried unsuccessfully to kick me off his pants leg. I intended to kill him! I couldn't control my rage. That urge to kill him remained inside me for years.

It was a few years later when he came to the door once more, pounding and shouting, demanding to be let in. That was when Ma became the powerful Mama Pig.

"You stay there under the covers!" We were all three in the one big bed under the red wool blanket that must have been part of Dad's Army gear. He continued to yell, banging harder on the door. Ma made it clear she was not going to open it.

"Then I'll break it down!" And he almost did. The door cracked. Ma got out of bed and picked up a baseball bat as she went to the door. Was the bat behind the old piano in the unfinished room? That's where I saw it years later.

Ma assured us, "He can huff, and he can puff, but he's not going to break down our door." What she said to him then made her my hero forever.

"You put your hand inside that door, and I'll knock it off!" She meant it, and he must have seen the bat through the crack. She stood right there waiting for his hand to reach through for the knob. It didn't happen. He left, never to return until we were adults.

Dorothy at early 12 Ellen Street

***

Way back then, the big black cast iron stove burned coal and wood until eventually Ma was able to have it converted to kerosene like Gram's stove. It was in the part of the first floor cordoned off by sheets of cardboard that had been nailed to the upstairs beams to retain heat. Keeping us warm was just one of the things Mama Pig did to keep us safe. In the winter, she put bricks on the back of the stove, tucking them into small flannel sacks to slide into the bottom of our bed. To go upstairs, we climbed a ladder. One half of the upstairs floor was not finished, and you could see or drop down to the first floor. Before there were windows up there, Ma had to go up to shovel the snow so it wouldn't melt and drip downstairs. Water was a big problem. In winter, we could melt snow we brought inside from right next to the door. In warm weather, we'd go over to Mark Hays' pond with big aluminum jugs. It was a long walk. Later, we got a rain barrel that caught rainwater from the roof. Mosquitos would lay eggs that hatched into little twitching worms. Kerosene was dropped in to smother the larvae, and that water was used for everything except for drinking. Eventually, our good neighbors, the Millett's, let us draw water from their outside silcock.

We added a tall cupboard with lots of drawers, a slide out enamel top, a storage bin for flour, and doors above with shelves. It was my favorite piece of furniture, and Ma painted bright parrots on the upper doors. We had a kitchen table, and Ma glued the rungs of kitchen chairs to make them sturdy. We girls slept on a pull-out couch bed. There was a door leading into the cardboard wall portion of the ground floor. The exit door we used was in that unfinished half and led to the backyard. There were wooden steps, and then you turned right around the side and passed the cellar door

14

before you got to the front yard. There was a trap door to the cellar inside the unfinished room a few feet from that door. I forgot and left it open once, and Audrey stepped in when the house was dark and dropped the seven or eight feet onto the ledge below. She didn't break any bones, but she never forgave me for laughing. It was so terrifying, hearing her drop and disappear. I didn't then understand fear and terror that causes hysterical laughter. We kids did a lot of climbing and jumping, like out of the other door that had no steps. Darkness was another problem. There was no electricity in the house. We used kerosene lamps.

Early 12 Ellen Street #2

Because there was no water, we also did not have a bathroom or a toilet. The first outhouse was up on the banking outside the back door. When it filled up, we dug a new pit up on the hill out in back. The last one was low to the right of the back door. They were all far enough away from the house that night trips were formidable. At night, we used a slop pail that rested on a low box.

Digging new pits and moving the outhouse was another of Mama Pig's admirable engineering feats. We helped her dig, then tipped it flat, holding it steady as Ma put long pipes horizontally under the front and middle, switching them back to front as it rolled to the new spot. She taught us how to lay a tongue-and-groove hardwood floor, too. That was when we were preparing to make the unfinished half livable. Not having electricity or running water meant we also had few childhood friends play at our house: just the Jones girls. They were brown like us. Even when relatives came to visit, mostly from Cape Cod and Boston, they stayed at 6 Ellen Street, where Gram and Gran'pa lived.

When Audrey started Roosevelt School, Dad was still around. The teachers knew us as Jan's grandchildren. Gran'pa was the school's janitor, and the bigger kids knew him from raising homing pigeons. He was an expert on raising animals and helped the boys raise and train their pigeons. They called him Jan. If Dad brought Audrey to school late, the teachers were polite to the Captain. Once he was gone, however, they smacked her hands with a rattan stick for tardiness. When I got to go to school, we ran our legs off trying to beat the bell. Ma wouldn't let us leave the house until the first bell had already rung, so we wouldn't be in the schoolyard where the nigger name calling was the worst. One morning, we heard the late bell ring just as we reached the school door. No more beating Audrey's hands with the ruler. We dashed back to Gram's house and hid in her outhouse until school was over. She had big bells on her screen door, and when we heard her coming, we dashed out and hid behind the outhouse. When school let out, we walked up the hill to our house, just like usual.

Being the Janitor's grandchildren was a proud thing. He died while we were still going to Roosevelt School. Ma stopped calling me names about that time. By then, I'd pretty much figured out that her mean name calling was her misguided attempt to toughen me up for the institutional racism I would surely encounter.

I began the journey of figuring out who I wanted to be.

Audrey and Shirley in the Snow circa 1934

CHAPTER 4

Looking Like Topsie

Growing up Colored in the early nineteen-thirties put dread in a young girl's heart. I would cringe when certain books and laundry products were anywhere in sight. Little Black Sambo and the Gold Dust Twins were the worst! Aunt Jemima baking products were not as disturbing, but Uncle Tom's Cabin *was in the same category. I never wanted to look at nor read such a book, not one about slavery. Even as an adult, my disdain for the book prevailed. Black men were ridiculed for being "Uncle Toms," implying that they were submissive and deferential, acting like victims in the presence of white people. And of course, Topsie, one of the girl characters in the dreaded book, was only one of many racial epithets tossed at me, including by my mother. Her mean behavior was painful and remains so even now. Yet I wonder if perhaps she was trying to keep me from looking like some kind of fool that white people would laugh at.*

Why would I ever want to read Uncle Tom's Cabin?" *Why? Because this novel made a most remarkable difference in the post-colonial, slave-owning country called the United States of America. My country! For decades, the selective history taught young people in these United States never included masterpieces like Harriett Beecher*

18

Stowe's _Uncle Tom's Cabin_. Yet the publication of Stowe's book in 1851-1852 helped to promote and expand the abolitionist movement.

It was quite by chance that I had the privilege of reading this inspirational and courageous piece of literature, based on real people and real issues. Lo and behold, at my youngest daughter's fiftieth birthday, she returned a book I had given her from my grandparents' house. When the house was torn down, I salvaged every book, letter and postcard I could lay my hands on. Among the books I had shared with her was a copy of Stowe's book: copyright 1893 by Houghton, Mifflin and Company, Boston and New York: The Riverside Press, Cambridge. The Brunswick Edition. It is a hardcover, small edition with a slim white spine and gold lettering on the red cover. It is in remarkable condition, and I read it in amazement. There are no illustrations, but I had already plenty of images in my mind before I turned the first page. It was my mother who had given me my picture of Topsie: an ugly black creature with wild unkempt braids all over her head. I knew I was being insulted when she called me that and was expected to clean myself up and tame my nappy head. I did not want to look like Topsie!

But these were not in Stowe's book at all. In truth, Topsie is a cunning, wild, savvy, abused, beaten and half-starved slave girl. She is rescued, mentored and ends up becoming a very successful resident of Maine. What a proud image! Uncle Tom is a principled, Christ-like character, forbearing and inspirational. In his life and his brutal death at the hands of Simon Legree, he gives witness to his fellow enslaved people of a true sense of freedom.

19

All of Beecher Stowe's characters are symbolic. Some are likenesses of people she knew or who were known by trusted resources. What impressed me most was her ability to amplify the good intentions and kindnesses that existed in the slave South in spite of horrific circumstances. She continually refers to the Bible, the church and the ironies found in the inter-relationships between religion and human bondage. American slavery was an unspeakable crime. All slavery is evil, yet the legally sanctioned and enforced atrocities of the American version are among the worst. Harriett Beecher Stowe encapsulates the attitudes, demonic circumstances and untenable situations both slave and slave owners endured. If you also have never considered reading it, dare yourself. You will recognize the remnants that continue to plague our society.

Shirley circa 1937

CHAPTER 5

Lee Heights

That's where I lived in my reveries: an enchanting place embedded in my memory by a woman who once dared to dream. Surely spirits inhabit the souls of the living. Images of unique beasts and a mélange of people somewhere on an island off the east coast of Africa entered me as a child.

In my mother's younger years, she was playful. In high spirits, she declared, "Lee Heights, that's what I'll call this place!" She could smile and dance and sometimes sang as she elevated her mood up and out of what looked like despair. This woman and her ancestors held onto and passed on dreams and fantasies. They whispered to this girl child. I became the Earl of Lee Heights: a powerful identity. I came from strong hearts and deep passions, unfettered by harsh realities.

My maternal grandmother also held onto hopes and dreamed of a beautiful home. The temporary shelter her husband built for her was the only home she had at her life's end. "I'm going to the Hollow," she'd say in the cloudy confusion of age, too much insulin and too little food sending her to a familiar, significant place like the Hollow on Cape Cod where she had spent so much of her life.

It matters naught that some little girls' dreams don't come true. What is vital, what is true about us women, the girl, the mother, the grandmother and all ancestors back to Guinea, Madagascar, Bermuda and the plantation in Maryland is: we dared to dream!

My grandfather planned, focused, found work, bought land and fulfilled yearnings. My grandmother planned, hoped and stored her wedding gifts, awaiting a more permanent home. Her beautiful china was stored in a hot attic; her silver engraved napkin rings, linens and her wedding invitation rested in a shed. Some were rescued by her granddaughters when the shed was broken into and the sturdy temporary home was bulldozed in order to build a new home for one of her great-granddaughters.

My grandmother had already stored priceless gifts of courage from her own mother. Her mother, illiterate, brave, a vessel of hope, steeped in the spirit of those who came before her, walked into an unknown future on an unfamiliar secret underground railroad. Her journey continued the journey of the generation before her: the horrid middle passage across the ocean on a slave ship. Yet it was known to her. All memory is stored, held onto and passed on in spirit women.

Life for me was not easy, yet I could never say it better than Maya Angelou, in her poem, "Still I Rise":

Still I Rise

—Maya Angelou

...I'm a black ocean, leaping and wide,
Welling and swelling I bear in the tide.

Leaving behind nights of terror and fear
I rise
Into a daybreak that's wondrously clear
I rise
Bringing the gifts that my ancestors gave,
I am the dream and the hope of the slave.
I rise
I rise
I rise

CHAPTER 6

The Earl of Lee Heights

It might seem peculiar, a little girl considering herself an Earl: a person of royal bearing, gentry, perhaps a title bestowed by the queen. It fit perfectly in my dream world: that place my imagination created while living in the peculiar house on Ellen Street. It was my mother, my queen, who dubbed the house "Lee Heights."

I'm convinced children world-wide, if given a chance, use imagination to transport themselves as far away as they wish. Imagination is wonderful fodder for creativity and the engine that drives dreams. I was also a lover of legends. One of my favorites was the missionary story. It explained where my maternal grandfather's ancestors came from. You see, there were three men from Guinea who entered the United States with missionary names: Meshach, Eshack and Abednego. At immigration, they re-named themselves Elias, Edward and Francis. Perhaps the family sir name was already Rickards, but the legend concludes with the fact that my grampa was named after his father and both uncles: Elias Edward Francis Rickards. I know Grampa was born in Boston in 1867, and his name truly was Elias Edward Rickards. On the birth record, Grampa's father is identified as Edward Rickards. I was told that both he and my grandmother, his wife, had the middle name Francis—and that's where my middle name came from. It seems the spelling changes for girl babies. The letter I becomes an E.

My paternal ancestors came from the British West Indies, specifically, Barbados. I knew both grandfathers. My father's father, Joseph Nathan Barrow, was living in Bermuda when I visited him. That visit was a dream fulfilled. For many years, letters, postcards and shells came to our house in Worcester, Massachusetts from Bermuda. There was a family legend about how he left the U.S.

It had occurred after a disagreement over where the family was to live. His wife, Annie, wished to leave the countryside of Southborough, MA and move into the City of Boston. He refused and informed his wife if she dared to take his children into the city, he would leave and never return. I was told that it was true; he never returned. His sons, my father the second oldest, always kept contact with their father, and Dad was given his father's seamen's carpenter tool chest, which I now possess. My father's oldest sister, Anna Dena, assured me that she never saw her father again and wistfully asked if I had taken a photograph of him while I was in Bermuda. I had. She gazed at the photo for a long time. It seems that the legend was a true story: a sad story. It was this aunt, Anna, who told me about her and my father's maternal grandmother, Matilda Belt. As a young one, Anna had been told that this grandmother was an Indian. It made Anna proud. Being an Indian was so much better than being a Negro. When Anna had the opportunity, she inquired about her grandmother's tribe. With great pride, Grandmother Belt informed Anna that she was a Madagascar Indian. Never having heard of that tribe, Anna looked up Madagascar and found it was off the east coast of Africa. Anna never again spoke with pride about her maternal grandmother, the Madagascan Indian, a Malagasy. I felt sad. I was a very young woman at the time, and I knew the sting of being identified as a person with ancestors from the "Dark Continent." That spurred classmates to call you a "jungle bunny" and a few other unsavory names. Studying about Africa was an ugly ordeal for Colored children of the past. Today, the Madagascar heritage intrigues me. I don't want it to be another legend.

My hunger for prideful identity as well as a bit of immature embarrassment inspired me to write a legend. It came at an invitation of a colleague. "Write a story about something troubling, and give it a positive or triumphant ending," Ted instructed. "Just make something up." I had already begun to sign all creative works "Eolh," or the Earl of Lee Heights, and so I immediately had my main character.

The Village: A Fairy Tale

Once upon a time there was a griot known throughout the village for her splendid memory and gift of forethought. How could any of them have known that her precognition was as accurate as her amazing memory?

"Eolh," the children would say, "tell me again what my grandchildren will say of me?" They giggled at the prospect of actually being as withered and sage as old Eolh and rolled with laughter to imagine themselves having grandchildren. Eolh would smile gently and then

26

with great seriousness insist upon a specific question from just one of the svelte, brown, wriggling urchins at her feet.

"Me, me first!" bid the oldest of the girls: a stunning bud of a woman with fierce eyes and untamed locks that receded greatly due to her massive forehead. Her hair crowned her head much like a lion's mane. She pleaded, "I am most in need of the future. My days are numbered before the ceremony of women." The fire in her eyes and the strength of her voice assured those who knew her that she could easily endure the torturous rites of passage that sent some girls into dumb submissiveness for the rest of their lives. Her name was Lasha, and her request was granted without question. The younger children admired her and longed to have her power, bordering on intimidation but tamed with humor. Lasha could make a wild beast curious with her impish boldness. She could imitate any bird or beast of the deep woods with sound or motion. Even Eolh would have to listen closely to Lasha's sounds to determine if it was a parrot, come to rest near her hut, or Lasha perfecting a new sound.

Eolh closed her eyes while she rested her hands on the girl's shoulders. Lasha's muscles rippled with tension. The solemn face of Eolh summoned feelings of awe in the young girl. A great shiver went up her spine and a wave of gooseflesh travelled along the muscles of her arms.

Eolh began, "I see two grandchildren, both boys. They wear the paint of hunters and bear the scars of a ritual unknown to this humble village. One prepares to follow the stars on the sea to a faraway place where lies a rumbling mountain. He is neither pompous nor proud, but a wise mariner. He leaves the land that juts into the sea like a big foot, and the great mountain spews ash deeper than our tallest trees. It is your grandson who brings produce hewn by the hand, not harvested from our soil. These are the tales he will tell you and others of our sleepy village."

"What new foods can be hewn by hand beyond that which is from bow and spear, old one?" Lasha asked.

"Ah," answered Eolh. "You will enjoy cooking in pots of fired mineral instead of clay, and wear necklaces and woven cloth. Not hide but a softer spun mantle will grace these priestess shoulders."

"Me, a priestess? Oh Eolh, you do not joke with me, do you? It is I who laugh at the wind. Tell me more!"

Eolh opened her eyes and smiled admiringly at the child as if she were already adorned. Lasha's taunting request was interrupted from a loud demand from among the lolling children.

Eshack, the smallest of them, boomed in a surprisingly loud voice, "Tell me now! It is I who has the name of the God men who came to our village. It is I who must hear the voice of the time to come. The pale medicine men say I will never die. Surely, I will speak with many, many grandchildren and great-grandchildren!"

Although Eshack had wriggled before her, Eolh had to gaze down from her hide-covered stool to meet his eyes: so tiny was his firm body, perfectly proportioned, the color of soil. The old griot hesitated as if unsure that this small soul could carry the burden of so many tomorrows. She gently stroked his head, a spongy cushion of tightly coiled charcoal ringlets.

Solemnly, she revealed to him, "Eshack, your grandchildren will never return to tell you their stories."

Eshack swooned, and his eyes became glittering pools of darkness as they brimmed with tears. "Never, never come back? But, Eolh, where can they go? The sea returns all it doesn't swallow."

The Old One touched his cheek as one unruly tear beaded and dashed down his face, leaving a hair-like rivulet that vanished before it reached his chin. His need to know danced through his whole body, causing him to wriggle and move against her knees. He wedged himself, fixing his eyes on her withered face.

"Why, Eolh," he demanded, "why do they not return?"

Half to calm him and to prepare him for the long tomorrows, she promised him, "Eshack, I will speak for your grandchildren and tell you their story. One will bear your name and master the waters beyond the sea that we know. He will not hunt but one day carry a great torch of fire into a large clearing for great games of strength and courage. This place will be warm and have great high stone huts with great trees to adorn them. Men like those who gave you your name will place a circle of dark leaves upon his head. A swifter runner will be hard to find. Another grandson will cross the big water to a place where mist turns to pellets like beating sand upon drying hide. He, too, will carry a missionary name and have many children, all of whom will look like you, their grandfather. These children will walk on grey stone and red soil and long black mats covering the soil. Their feet will be covered with smooth hide, and their eyes will be deep pools like yours. Their questions will be as loud and urgent as yours are today. They must look for you, little Eshack. They seek your ashes in order to know who they really are. Yes, one comes in my vision: a *great-great-grandchild.*"

Impatiently, Eshack asks, "What is his story for me? You must tell me, or I will never know."

In answer to his plea, the Old One crooned, "Ah, yes, this is a girl child with a name never spoken in our time. She is called 'Shirley,' and she asks only to know you, Eshack. You must live your life well so the next hundred griots can tell your story, that she might know who you are."

Eshack stood tall, staring at his lanky shadow stretching taller than his tiny self. For a long while, he pondered what he had been told and then announced: "I will be the next griot of this village and see to it that all grandchildren will know **all** of us forevermore!"

CHAPTER 7

All Things Bright and Beautiful

To dream anything that you want to dream, that is the beauty of the human mind. To do anything that you want to do, that is the strength of the human will. To trust yourself, to test your limits, that is the courage to succeed.

—Bernard Edmonds

Who gets to live their dreams? Perhaps before Eleanor Roosevelt's amazing example of what women can aspire to and accomplish, most women in my growing up years expected to be good wives and mothers. Those dreaming about careers welcomed the prospect of becoming teachers, secretaries or perhaps nurses. It was just the way the world was in yesteryears. My young girl dream was to be an aviatrix or an eye surgeon. I had always wanted to fly like a bird, a dream that didn't come true for many years. Eyes also fascinated me; as a teenager, I signed up to donate my eyes to the Boston Eye Bank after death. Before those dreams became serious, I wanted to be a boy. There was something alluring about being loud, strong and bold. A quiet girl, I envied such attributes, knowing being a boy was an impossible dream.

Parents and teachers did not ask me what I aspired

to be when I grew up. My mother assumed I would clean houses, tend children or run an elevator. Those were the jobs available to her. She had other jobs, too, like sewing men's trousers for the Works Progress Administration (WPA) under Franklin D. Roosevelt's New Deal. She hated that job. It was her serious suggestion that I not waste time going to high school. I listened, but I held onto my own dreams, steadfastly expecting that the time would come when all things would be bright and beautiful. It was one of the hymns we sang in church that instilled hope. Children remain hopeful as long as they are permitted to have dreams.

My expectation of good things became tempered by repeated disappointments, but like the optimistic boy who discovers only a pile of dung under the Christmas tree, I was certain that meant there had to be a pony somewhere. Psychologists explain dispositions and differences in children by noting opposite reactions to identical hardships and challenges. One child will collapse in despair while the other holds onto a spark of hope that something good may eventually happen. I was the latter kind of child.

We worry about what a child will become tomorrow, yet we forget he is somebody today.
—Stacia Tauscher.

Good things did come my way. Early on, it was the strong alliance I made with the sister I grew up with. Later in life, it was good friends and neighbors who kept the spark alive. Graduations were beautiful happenings for me, and birthdays were always special.

When I graduated from junior high school, the whole class went on a cruise to Provincetown, Massachusetts. We gathered early in the morning at Foster's Wharf in Boston, spent four hours at sea, four hours ashore on the very tip of Cape Cod, then four more hours return on the boat. Fantastic!

My mother never showed joy working for a living. The particular dream she shared that I remember was her wish to be an interior decorator, perhaps because she dreamed of creating beauty in our half-finished house. My first paid jobs were a joy to me, yet Audrey hated them. Tending chickens was *my* job at home, and I sold fresh eggs to neighbors. Audrey and I were also commissioned by our mother to sell handcrafts to the neighbors. Ma, her sister, Evelyn, and our grandmother crocheted fancy handkerchiefs and doilies, and Ma sewed stuffed animals. It was exciting to me to make a sale. My sister was mortified. Knocking on doors, having people repeatedly say "No, thank you" or slam the door in our faces, upset her. I relished the opportunity and had regular customers who bought my eggs. We never spent the money we earned, but immediately gave it to our mother to use for the household expenses.

Entering nursing school was another bright and beautiful event in my life. We were paid a stipend: ninety dollars a month, with sixty deducted for board and room, and so we each had thirty dollars. Audrey and I gave half to our mother.

It seems sad to me when a friend or colleague tells me how much they hate their job. Thankfully, I never had that experience. There were hateful incidents, such as difficult supervisors or frightening events, but those were never enough to make me hate the job itself.

In the 1950s, I was working at Georgetown University Hospital, a teaching hospital in Washington D.C. where I planned to earn my bachelor's degree in nursing. The program that attracted me combined work and study schedules designed to allow a nurse to earn her degree. It never happened. The Georgetown hospital contracted with the Catholic University, which did not accept Black students. Alternate arrangements would require me to travel to Maryland, and the "Learn and Earn" program Georgetown offered would not be available to me.

The worst recollection from my working life came from an event that occurred when I was assigned to the hospital's maternity ward. This is ordinarily a joy-filled nursing duty, on a floor where things are most often bright and beautiful. On this day, however, a new admission was sitting in her room waiting to be seen by the obstetrician when she had a spontaneous fatal heart attack. The obstetrician came, scalpel in hand, ripped open her dress and lacerated her from chest to pelvis, delivering a bloody, howling, healthy baby boy. The distraught father could not look at nor hold his son. It was an unforgettable, horrible day.

Whether working in a hospital, home health agency or neighborhood center, in Washington D.C., Maine or Massachusetts, I found joy in my work. There were many years I worked in public schools and a few more years in college. Teaching young people and young adults was intense, low-paying and overly burdened by paperwork. There were always challenges, yet the joy of working with young people is priceless.

My own experience as a student at Grafton Street

Junior High had been positive, and my teachers had been creative and supportive. I especially remember my eighth grade English teacher, who was the first person to show me that my love of writing was useful and could be shared with others. I wrote a story about a fire, and he read it aloud to the class. Everyone was gripped. When he finished, he said, "*This* is writing a story."

My joy was multiplied when I ended up teaching in that same school. By then, it had been renamed Worcester East Middle School. My students were curious, inventive and eager to learn about health. When I acquired CPR mannequins from the Army Reserve, both a baby and an adult, some eighth graders decided to become certified to teach CPR. I was able to do many such hands on classes. I invited guests, showed films while allowing students to run the projector and had them do presentations about health heroes. My most rewarding experience involved my practice of "contracting" for grades. Students chose the grade they wanted and honored the terms of their contracts, often renegotiating in favor of the more demanding requirements for a B or an A. The only way to fail my health and safety class was to be chronically absent. That never happened.

Several events in my life not related to work brought absolute joy. One involved a money booth. A new branch bank was opening in the grocery store where I shop. Customers were given envelopes with a key inside. If your key opened the gate where the bank and booth were set up, you entered and joined the line of other lucky shoppers waiting their turn to enter the booth. It had four clear Lucite walls and was the size of a phone booth. Once inside, an air vent flooded the booth with real bills: single dollars and some fives. You could keep all you could grab. It was exhilarating. I laughed hysterically and had money resting on my head along with two handfuls of folding money. One young girl just stood, not reaching or grabbing. She leaned her butt against the booth and cradled her hands together, just smiling while the money whirled around her. When the air flow stopped, she hugged the money that had fallen into her hands, reached behind her to grab the pile that accumulated there, and ran to her parents, screaming with delight. She had more money than all the adults!

There were to be other events of peak brightness and beauty in my life, not least the thrill of learning to fly a propeller airplane, soaring on thermals in a glider and floating serenely in a hot air balloon above the countryside. Indeed, these and lesser events ranged beyond my childhood hopes and dreams. I am blessed to be one of those children who never gave up hope, always expecting that good things would eventually come my way.

CHAPTER 8

Ten-Yard Roller

Dr. Maroney was often whistling as he burst through the swinging doors of the Winslow Surgery at Worcester City Hospital. He was five foot ten at most: trim, erect and driven, with handsome ruddy features and a confident stride. We first met when I was eighteen years old and in training as a scrub nurse. Miss Kendall, the supervisory nurse in the operating room, held high expectations for all of the students she trained. She did not base her opinion on what one might consider promising or exceptional performance. Her method was to have students with skills she trusted work with surgeons who were specialists in their fields. Specialists typically brought their own scrub nurses to hospitals, nurses they had trained and trusted with the expensive, imported instruments unique to their respective fields. In contrast, Miss Kendall would only allow City Hospital nurses in her OR (operating room), and she had the backing of the administration. She singled me out to be one of the best, as she had with my sister, Audrey, who is very intelligent, talented and has extraordinary fine motor skills.

It is difficult to imagine Miss Kendall in street clothes or with a smile on her face. A white cotton scrub cap covered her nondescript hair; white cotton gauze masked the bridge of her nose and was tied behind her ears and under her chin. Her bony body was fully draped in a white sterile gown wrapped tightly around her waist, and her hands were always in tan rubber gloves. All nurses wore white shoes in the nineteen forties, and we students were "gowned and gloved" like Miss Kendall when we assisted surgeons. Miss Kendall was known for her expert skills and judgment.

She was confident that her chosen students would be as good or perhaps better than those trained by the surgeons. Perhaps we were, but my skills were not the same as my sister's! I was the daughter not allowed to use the Singer sewing machine. I broke needles. The darned machine would go backwards as I worked the treadle. My fine motor skills were perhaps average. It was my sister, Audrey, who mastered embroidery at the tender age of five, not me. While in grade school, she trimmed the toes of our diabetic grandfather. That was her job, and she was excellent. Comparing one child to another can leave one feeling less than or inferior. I grew up feeling less than.

Without this knowledge of my reputation, Miss Kendall chose me to work with Dr. Smith, the plastic surgeon. His instruments were miniatures, handcrafted in Switzerland. I assisted the brain surgeon, Dr. Carmody. His instruments were made in Germany and could not be autoclaved (sterilized in ovens using high pressure and steam). The sharp drills had to penetrate bone and required soaking in special sterilizing solutions; held by sterile tools, they were then carefully, strategically, placed on the instrument table, known as the "lap table." The scrub nurse set up the instrument tables. They were long, chest high, stainless steel tables covered with layers of sterile white tablecloths adorned with sponges, sutures, scalpels, snaps, kokas, retractors and clamps. They all had special names, places and uses—and the scrub nurse had best know each name and purpose! Confusing a Kelly clamp with a koka clamp, which has sharp teeth, would be catastrophic.

The brain surgeon used special little Styrofoam-looking pledgets threaded with a loop of black silk to sponge blood. He plucked them from my gloved hand. Many patients were awake, sitting upright in a chair as at the dentist. I never trembled. When preparing to assist, my head and hands were sure and steady. It wasn't until just before surgery, when everything was prepared, that my stress level would peak. My intestines convulsed, and I got diarrhea. I would have to leave the blazing bright operating theater and, on my return, re-scrub, re-gown, put on fresh gloves and bravely step up on the stool that gave me command of the entire instrument array. This embarrassing ritual never upset Miss Kendall. She always allotted me plenty of time to set up my table. I expected to be thrown out or, at least, removed from the elite group of scrub nurses. But I assisted all of the specialists, learning about their particular instruments and adhering to their protocols.

My encounter with John Maroney, the thoracic surgeon, was most memorable. Surgeons, cutting into the chest cavity, deal with large blood vessels that occasionally burst, sending a jet stream of blood to the ceiling. The chest cavity fills with blood, obscures the damaged vessel and makes it impossible to clamp it. Death is imminent. I was assisting Maroney when such a disaster occurred.

He yelled, "GET ME A TEN-YARD ROLLER!"

A what? I knew my instruments, but I had no idea what a ten-yard roller was. He quickly explained. It was a flannel roll made especially for him and was kept in a sterile canister on the cabinet behind me.

"Grab that can and toss the roller over here!"

"But I'm scrubbed in," I replied meekly. To get the canister, I would have to break scrub, contaminating my gloves and gown.

"Eckie!" I called in panic for Miss Ecknoian, the circulating nurse.

But Dr. Maroney leaned toward me, thrust his elbow into my chest and knocked me off the stool onto my butt. "Now you're not sterile! Grab that can!"

Miss Ecknoian had heard his first shout. She ran in, grabbed the can and tossed the roller onto the surgical field while simultaneously grabbing me off the floor by the scruff of my neck, whipping off my gown and gloves and re-gowning and re-gloving me! In seconds, I was back on the stool, watching the amazing properties of a ten-yard roller save a patient from certain death.

I admired Dr. Maroney, and I believe he took a keen interest in me that day. My sister and I were novelties: the first Black students admitted to the Worcester City Hospital School of Nursing. When this man asked for something, even something as simple as, "What is my patient's blood pressure?" I knew better than say, "I don't know." I had seen other nurses and interns make that mistake. Maroney would explode. I do not recall his swearing, but he would call you every incompetent, degrading name imaginable. His loud voice would announce to everyone how stupid and worthless you were in his eyes.

After graduation, I worked in Winslow Surgery. In the 1800s, it had been the main surgery: a large amphitheater, with balcony seats and several small surgical rooms. By now, at the end of the 1940s, only minor surgery and procedures not requiring anesthesia were done here, along with burn dressings and debridement as well as the application and removal of orthopedic plaster casts. Maroney's patients were awake, swallowing dilators to open scarred windpipes; he also treated epistaxis: severe nose bleeds.

The Winslow Surgery nurses and Emil, the orthopedic aide, would literally run out of sight when Maroney burst through those swinging doors. I often found myself alone when he arrived. Whatever question he asked, I would beam at him, and if I did not have the answer, I would cheerfully say, "I'll find that out for you." I was the official warm greeter. He knew I liked him and appreciated his work. It went both ways.

He admired my sister and me. He wondered about my culture. He did not ask the veiled racist question: the "What are you?" question, followed by, "Where are you from? Are you Canadian?" As a young person, it struck me as a strange question, and I would answer, "I'm American." Later, I understood that it really meant, "you're not like other Black people I know." It annoyed me. It also implied that I did not speak Black English. Black English was not allowed in my house. John Maroney was curious about how removed I was from my ancestral roots. My absence of Black culture intrigued him. He spoke and understood Swahili. I knew nothing about Africa and its many cultures. It

41

pleased him to give me a Swahili nickname, *Skokien*. He called my sister, *Tondeleo*. Many professionals at the hospital feared him. Some hated him. Our mutual respect endured.

There came a time when I asked him the meaning of the nicknames. "Oh," he answered, "*Todoleo* means beautiful flower, and *Skokien* is bubbling hooch... homemade brew." It made me laugh recalling the many times he called me *Skokien*!

NEW NURSES

Miss Shirley F. Barrow (left) and Miss Audrey E. Barrow, June graduates from City Hospital School of Nursing, who were honored at dinner given last night by Civic Affairs Committee. The sisters leave for Germany soon.

FIRST NEGRO GRADUATES OF CITY HOSPITAL FETED

Miss Shirley F. Barrow and Miss Audrey E. Barrow, daughters of Mrs. Dorothy L. Barrow, 12 Ellen street, were honored last night at a dinner in Putnam and Thurston's.

They were June graduates from City Hospital School of Nursing. They are the first Negroes ever to graduate from the local hospital.

Immediately after the dinner, they left for New York and a trip to Germany where they will visit their father, Lt. Col. Benjamin T. Barrow, stationed with the U. S. forces in Stuttgart.

Speakers were Mayor Holmstrom, Theodore Austin, superintendent of Belmont and City Hospitals, Miss Mary T. Loftus, supervisor of nurses at City Hospital; Dr. John F. Curran Sr., City hospital surgeon; Miss Lillian Kohl, City Hospital student nurse advisor; George A. Wells, city councillor, and Dr. John J. Goldsberry, of the Civic Adams Committee.

Diocese to Sponsor Retreat For Scouts

Worcester Diocese will sponsor its first retreat for Catholic Boy Scouts Sept. 12-14 at Wachusett Council, Camp Wanocksett, Dublin, N. H.

Religious services will be conducted each day. Activities will include crafts, swimming, sports, movies and a campfire. Scouts have been asked to make reservations with their parish priests not later than Monday.

Rev. Robert T. Donahue is chaplain for scouting in Catholic churches of the Wachusett Council. It is expected the program will be repeated each year.

Shirley & Audrey 1952

It was much later in my life when I became seriously curious about my roots. I joined the New England branch of the Afro-American Historical and Genealogical Society (AAHGS). At a convention, I found one of the plenary speakers especially endearing. This very talented Black woman was in a mixed marriage and had a biracial daughter. She and her husband spent precious time talking to their child about the silly racist questions she was bound to face. When they got to the "what are you" question, they gently informed their child that this was a silly question, and she was not obliged to answer.

It happened sooner than they expected and within hearing distance of the parents. They were pleased and surprised to see their daughter smile brightly at the person and answer with great confidence and poise. "What am I? I am a butterfly and a song." Children have a wonderful respect for silly stuff.

It was at this same convention where I attended a program about DNA and tracing one's ancestral roots to the continent of Africa. There was a door prize: a free $100 personal DNA kit, including swab, analysis, the real thing. Guess who won? And shouted so loudly that folks who were not even in the auditorium heard the news? This author's matrilineal DNA informed her that she is a member of the Ticar people, who originated in the area now known as Cameroon. It is amazing to discover who you are genetically.

At times our own light goes out and is rekindled by a spark from another person. Each of us has cause to think with deep gratitude of those who have lighted the flame within us.

—Albert Schweitzer

CHAPTER 9

Love Letters

To write a love letter we must begin without knowing what we intend to say and without knowing what we have written.

—Jean-Jacques Rousseau

He was six-foot-three, dark and handsome. She was enthralled by his voice: the southern drawl and his gentlemanly manners. This was a match not made in heaven but by Dad.

"These are two young men I'd like you to meet. They are attending Howard with me. They're ambitious fellows, from a good family in Alabama."

The Colonel had handpicked young soldiers he entrusted to escort his daughters around the base when they visited him in Germany. The dating in Stuttgart was a pleasurable adventure, one of a kind for these young ladies from New England.

Dad, the Colonel, was now retired from the Army and along with these young veterans, was benefitting from the GI Bill, earning degrees at Howard University in Washington, D.C.

The courting did not quite go as planned. The expectation was for the younger brother to date the younger sister, then pair the two older siblings.

45

Miss Shirley, the younger, enjoyed the company of the younger brother, Mr. Taid (as "Ted" was pronounced in Alabama). The thick southern drawl was her only challenge.

Then Miss Audrey, big sister, declared, "You date the older one. He's no match for me!"

Miss Shirley found dating brother number two, Mr. OD, interesting as well. His military experience was with a special division of Black paratroopers, trained to jump into enemy territory, reconnoiter, report and destroy impediments for ground troop arrival.

"How were you supposed to meet up with the ground troops?" Miss Shirley asked in wonder.

"Oh, that was not part of the mission. We were on our own," Mr. OD responded with great pride.

One more date after the exchange of brothers, and Miss Audrey made her final choice. "The younger is no match for me, either. Take whichever one you want."

Well, take them she did. Mr. Taid became Miss Shirley's generous brother-in-law and Mr. OD her husband, Mr. Oscar Carter.

Miss Audrey later managed to date another young veteran from Virginia: a true southern gentleman to whom Miss Shirley introduced her after dating young men from Camp Devens, the army camp near their home in New England. Mr. Ernie also became her brother-in law. It took a few years and the exchange of many love letters for Miss Audrey's and Mr. Ernie's dating to mature into matrimony.

Postmark: North Virginia 18 November 1987
Letterhead stationery from:
Old Towne Child Development Center
721 North Columbus Street, Alexandria, VA 22314

Addressed to:
Ms. Shirley F. Carter
10 Westdale Street. Worcester, MA 01604

Dear Shirley,

Even as I write this letter, I have already sent Mia a few dollars. In order to assist her, I will do so on a regular basis.

I might add how wonderful you sound. I had forgotten how thrilled I have always been to hear you speak.

And, I won't forget Laura's birthday. I hope she won't be offended if I address her this way until

I learn her new name, proper spelling, etc.

Let's keep in touch.

> *Love,*
> *Oscar*

P.S. Picture was taken last fall

I saved this letter, and perhaps I even answered it. It is clear that we did not keep in touch. There are few letters saved. He may have actually contacted his daughters, but I will never know. My daughters rarely heard from their father and his "intentions" to send "a few dollars...on a regular basis" never happened. Four years after this letter, I wrote a letter to Oscar. I hope I mailed it. The copy I have was perhaps my draft, a thoughtful first attempt. There is also a possibility that it was written as a therapeutic gesture following the death of his mother. I'd like to believe I actually mailed it.

Oscar D. Carter 1987

August 5, 1991

Dear Oscar:

This letter is long overdue. For years it seems, I longed to unravel the mystery of your leaving. If only this or that had not happened, the wide-eyed wondrous girl-woman would still be your wife. It seems I was searching for answers to questions that had never been asked.

Why in God's name did you marry me? What drove you from one woman to another...even while we were married? Those questions you might ask yourself. What this letter is about is my telling you what's real, factual, and current with me. Our early life together is history: simple facts, compounded by complex times, distressed responses, immaturity, and different understandings of responsibility and commitment.

No longer do I blame myself. Whatever was missing or went amiss was not my singular undertaking. When facts are unknown, the mind "fills in the blanks." It no longer matters what happened to the four of us thirty-two years ago. We are different people now.

Please know that I loved you. I still love you. This letter is simply my goodbye. It's way past time for me to get on with my life. Raising our daughters took all the psychic and physical energy I could muster. It was a labor of love and I sought help all along the way. Most times, I got the assistance I needed. My life schedule was always jammed; full of childcare, jobs, extended family, church, and whatever noble endeavor I could find to fill the void. The emptiness I felt was a construct: a weird non-explanation for what went wrong. I'm exploring and discovering what's important in my life. My life is ever expanding. There was a blank space that I just let go... like an air bubble in a long narrow tube of fluid.

Some appreciations are due. I thank you for your efforts, past and present. I'm not sure why you sent the snapshots from your mom's house, but I enjoyed them and will share them with Laura and Mia. It was special being with you and your family, saying final farewells to Effie May. You've sent a letter or two in the past. I hesitated to answer. It seemed there was nothing left to say.

Now I know what I need to say and it's goodbye. I fully expect that you will realize your goals in life and somehow regain or remain in touch with the alive, ambitious, fun loving person you really are. It would be a great gift if you could allow Laura and Mia to get to know the man I fell in love with...and recognize him as their father.

As this is not a business letter it will arrive at your home. You need not fear embarrassment nor repetition. There will be no other letters. You can reach Laura at the Westdale Street address temporarily. Mia has relocated to Austin, Texas. You can reach her at 4108 Kilgore Lane, Austin, TX 78727, tel # 512-3397601.

Both daughters are at crucial turning points in their lives right now. Do get in touch with them.

> *As ever,*
> *Shirley*

I did write another letter to Oscar. It was a consent form requesting permission to use the names and photographs of people mentioned in my memoir, which was soon to be published.

He never replied. His brother, Taid, did reply, and I called Ted to get Oscar's current address.

"Why, Shirley, Oscar is dead." It was not what I was ready to hear. What I had hoped for was to hear the sound of Oscar's voice, which always made my heart leap: it sparked that amazing memory of once having been a loving wife, cherished by the handsome six-foot-three father of my wonderful daughters.

It was a wakeup call later when my older daughter nonchalantly accepted the news and declared, "I'll bet we're not even in his obituary." It seemed preposterous to me. Why wouldn't they be mentioned among those left behind? This internet savvy woman got me to confirm the date and place of Oscar's death: May 26, 2000 in Alexandria, Virginia. She got a copy of the Alexandria newspaper. I was mentioned as his first wife. In fact, I was his second wife, and the children he had abandoned in life were keenly aware that they would not be remembered at his death. They were *not* mentioned in his obituary.

Love letters: such interesting reminders of times long past.

Alas, writing this memoir has gotten me to go through old files. I put my hands on another letter from Oscar. It's dated 13 August 1991. It begins:

My dear Shirley,

You start out with the truth and end up with less clarity. Thank you for your letter, yes, it is long overdue. But to set the record straight, I did not leave you. The grounds for my divorce from you was desertion, that is, you deserted me and not I you. I married you because I loved you, you were the most beautiful and wonderful lady I had ever met. You fulfilled all of my fantasies. You were everything I wanted in a mate. You were my Mona Lisa, my Joan of Arc, my Virgin Mary and to top it all off, I loved your sense of humor and that voice. Let me add that you don't have to answer this letter..."

He continues in the next *five* pages to recount his ambition, his meeting and involvement with his next wives, and our meeting at his mother's funeral.

I did mail that letter. I actually was not sure.

CHAPTER 10

Sparrow

The smaller the head the bigger the dream.
—Eugene O'Neil

There was a time when I wanted to fly: get in an airplane and soar into the wild blue sky. The first time I heard about Lear jets and the possibility of buying one that could be assembled at home and then flown vertically out of your own backyard or field, I wanted one! I haven't yet met anyone who built their own jet from a kit, and Lear no longer gets much press, but flying? I had a wee taste.

It must have been my out loud dreaming about building a jet in the backyard or my raving to my family about how amazing flight was to me. Two gifts got me aloft: a glider ride and a hot air balloon ride. My sister, Audrey, and her children gave me these thrilling gifts. I needed companions as the rides were for two people; I assumed they were meant for both Audrey and me to enjoy. In my excitement, I forgot that she is terrified of heights and had no intention of joining me. My grand-nephew, Christopher, and my older daughter, Laura, were my flight companions: he in the glider and she in the hot air balloon.

The little bird flying in the sky first took on special

meaning for me when I was a young student nurse. I was called "Miss Sparrow" due to an auditory error. A coworker at Worcester City Hospital introduced me to a group of her friends. My maiden name is Barrow, and henceforth this group referred to me as "Miss Sparrow." I liked the moniker and use a version of it for my email address. I knew I would never be that little bird – but then I met Julian.

The meeting was again cleverly and lovingly engineered by my sister, Audrey, who is privy to all my dreams. We were at choral practice at Worcester State University. I had talked my sister into joining the chorus. We both enjoy singing, and I seduced her with what I had found to be true: no homework, no papers, just show up and sing! To my surprise, we had both homework and papers to write the semester that she joined, but that hard work culminated in an amazing professional performance of Mozart's *Requiem!*

It was in October, early in the semester, when she put a card into my hands before we took our seats in our voice range sections: me with the altos and she on the far right with the sopranos. It was sweet, and I suspect she alerted the student sitting beside her to watch me open what I had already guessed was my birthday card. Class started with attendance being taken, so there was plenty of time to open the card before we began. Inside was a small packet. I was gifted with a flying lesson at the Worcester Airport!

What? One can take a lesson and be instructed in how to fly in one day? Yes, indeed, and the instructor's name was Julian Suszanski. I am sure my face looked as if I had been stunned by a bolt of lightning. The scream I smothered stopped my breathing long enough

53

for my sister to grin boldly, eyes dancing in delight as she observed my near fainting condition.

I spent an entire day at the airport with Julian, a handsome twenty-three-year-old man with light brown hair. He instructed me in how to do safety checks on the two-seated Cessna, tether it properly and check water content in the oil mix. I read a brief safety manual, and by late afternoon I was moving quickly down the runway, throttle in hand!

Julian was calm, cool and relaxed as he instructed me to increase speed and pull hard on the throttle to clear the trees, confident that I would bring us into the wild blue sky. I did. He sat beside me, assuring me that he could take over if any event required it, but that I was free to fly all around Worcester County.

Flight School. Shirley in the Cockpit of Cessna

"Where do you want to go?" he asked.

"I want to fly over my house, my neighborhood."

Julian held the throttle while I took a photo of my house, and then we continued, passing over the many lakes we could see below. I have no sense of how long we were airborne. I was exhilarated. Coming in for the landing, I was able to angle into the wind, see the strip clearly and pull, pull hard, but the ground came up rapidly and the nose of the plane did not level in sync with our fast approach. Julian just smiled and asked if I wanted him to control the throttle. A quick, appreciative "Okay!" from me, and we were rolling smoothly along the runway.

With family gifts we do not always write thank you cards. I hope I sent one to Audrey. I know I sent one to Julian. I have the draft of the brief note.

Dear Julian,

This is a perfect time to thank you for the birthday gift you helped me enjoy this past October. My flight was wonderful: a childhood dream come true. No matter how I look at it, I feel very fortunate ... that you are talented and confident, and Whomever watches over you, also knows how precious you are.

Thanks, and best wishes,
Student, Shirley F.B. Carter

The year of my flight was 2003. A few months later, on February 26, 2004, the local newspapers carried a remarkable story. The headlines in the Worcester *Telegram & Gazette* read,

"Two unharmed in crash landing"
"Flight lesson out of city airport ends in field."

The article began, "A two-seat Cessna 152 landed belly up yesterday ... the pilot and student walked away unhurt."

Yes, it was my gifted, confident Julian, doing his very best.

CHAPTER 11

Stellar Events

It's not what you say out of your mouth that determines your life, it's what you whisper to yourself that has the most power.

—Robert Kiyosaki, entrepreneur

In the peaks and valleys of discovering not only who I am but all I could be, a few stellar events stand out. Among my many notes and middle-of-the-night jottings for this memoir, I rediscovered a list of experiences that I still consider beyond ordinary.

It's a varied array: The Salt Mine and Death Camp/Auschwitz in Poland; the three trips to Alaska; Poll Bearer/Rainy Day Funerals; Maestro/Bruce Miller; and the birth of the first great-grandchild.

The list begins with when I was an Olympic torch bearer in 1996, helping to pass the flame as it crossed the world from Greece to Atlanta, Georgia. Long before television, I had fallen in love with the Olympics: games devised to ward off war and champion tests of strength. And in my youth, I saw people who looked like me win gold medals! This admiration peaked first in 1980 with a trip to Los Angeles to attend the Summer Games. Tehran had declined to bid, and so Los Angeles was selected by default. The Olympics had been held there once before in 1932. This was a great opportunity for me and for my sister, Audrey, who shares my passion for the games, both summer and winter.

We bought tickets for track and field and a horseback riding event called dressage. I learned that dressage would not be a first-choice event. The object was for the rider to guide the horse so smoothly through a set of predetermined movements that it appeared effortless. It was incredibly boring, looking from the stands to see movements the riders were cleverly hiding. But just being at the Games was amazing. It was unbearably hot with very little smog, and we had an unforgettable adventure.

In 1996, when I discovered the Summer Olympics were again being held in the United States, this time in Atlanta, I silently wished I could carry the flame. There was a contest sponsored by United Way agencies across the country to enlist local heroes to carry the Olympic torch through their states. Applicants had to provide supporting and sponsoring letters describing how they had served their communities. It was still quite early in the year. I made inquiries, told people who knew of my community endeavors, procured the application forms and made my plea. Come October, I would be sixty-five years old and might never again have the opportunity to do the torch run. Several people including my daughter, Laura, and sister Audrey wrote on my behalf. I was chosen!

There were preparations and protocols, with uniforms to arrange and caveats about underwear and hair spray. Torch carriers had to be able to walk at least a kilometer, the distance between runners. The weight of the torch itself was about two pounds, similar to a wooden baseball bat. I practiced running the track at Lake Park to make sure I could manage the single kilometer, a bit longer than a half-mile distance.

The Olympic Torch Passing the Flame

It was a glorious sunny June day. A crowd of people lined the streets of Hudson, Massachusetts to see me run: My family; local friends; my friends, Eliane and Inés, who had come from Florida; out-of-town relatives; neighbors; a busload from my church; the members of my YWCA exercise class and our instructor; my international peer counseling folks—and no doubt others I have forgotten.

Technicians were assigned to open and close the

fuel valve of each torch, and all runners had escorts who would assist if we faltered or needed help. To my great surprise, we held on to our individual torches and only passed the flame. It is the privilege of Olympic medal winners to carry the torch whenever they chose. My flame came from an Olympic medal winner, and I flew up the hill to pass the flame to another Olympic medal winner. My adrenalin surged for hours after the run. I was interviewed, let young and old hold the torch for photos, the town videoed the entire event and a friend made a copy for me.

The golden moment came when I was in Texas at my daughter's house, regaling her and some friends about my adventure. I mentioned that the Olympic Committee invites torch relay runners to buy their torches for a few hundred dollars. I told them how much I would love to own the beautiful custom-made centennial torch, but it was much too expensive.[2] My daughter said, "How much?" and proceeded literally to pass a hat around the room! Bills filled the hat. I managed the balance, and the torch now hangs in an open case on my living room wall. It still has fuel and was fired at a family reunion at Camp Hale, New Hampshire the following year.

Unforgettable!

[2] *The 32-inch-high torch—the tallest for a Summer Olympic Games–is designed to resemble 22 reeds, one for each modern Olympic Games. The handle is made from Georgia hardwood. A gold band above the handle features the Atlanta 1996 logo and Quilt of Leaves motif. The name of each Olympic Games host city is etched on a gold band near the base of the torch.*

–John Dunn: *Georgia Tech Alumni: Magazine* , Vol 73, No 01 1996

CHAPTER 12

Courtroom

My free Legal Aid lawyer stood by my side. He was about my age, early thirties, and a rather non-descript, confident white male. He seemed unconcerned about this big ugly place. Entombed within a larger room, the courtroom had multiple doorways and tiny windows up near the ceiling. They did not appear to let in sunlight. The judge, robed in his formal black, stood above us behind a raised dais resting on a small platform, like a mini-stage. He held a gavel in his hand at all times. Clerks whispered and handed him papers, which he tossed back at them after a slam of the gavel. He never once looked at me, directing his attention only to my lawyer.

I surveyed the courtroom, a huge hall with a few empty back row chairs. I was looking for the love of my life, Oscar D. Carter. He had to be over there. I saw Richard Cook. Oscar and I had been friends with Richard and his wife when we were first married and lived in D.C. Richard had graduated from Howard University and was a bona fide lawyer. I stared right at him, and he looked away. His dark suit and somber expression made him a stranger. He was no longer my friend. He was Oscar's lawyer. But where was Oscar?

The Legal Aid lawyer remained relaxed as the judge

pounded the gavel and shouted, "Next case!" Why did he have to yell? Couldn't they give him a microphone? His face remained stern, matching the frightening sound of that damn gavel. Then the Clerk echoed him.

"Next case, Oscar D. Carter verses Shirley Carter in the matter of a Divorce."

Somewhere in that announcement, he used the word DESERTION. I turned numb. My eyes blurred, and I couldn't hear anything. How in God's name did I get here? Why did that word, desertion, make me hold my breath? Is this what it was like when people fainted? Anger flooded my brain, paralyzing my whole body. The gavel slammed again. The judge repeated, in angry tones, "Next case!" He sounded the way I felt: enraged!

My lawyer stood calmly beside me, waiting. Waiting for what? I could feel the perspiration soaking my armpits. At my mother's coaching, I wore a lovely print dress, a Sunday hat and gloves. Ma assured me, "This will influence the judge." What made her believe that? My mother had been to court multiple times. Her first divorce was from Bill Perkins. It was a nasty divorce, one involving children, custody, health issues and the death of their son, Lawrence. They had called him Sunny. Ma left her husband and children and went to her cousins' house in Leominster. She worked in a laundry there. Desertion? Did she indeed desert her husband and children?

I never deserted my husband.

Ma divorced my father, too. I'm sure *she* sued *him*. I was there when he left her. I spent hours with her in the lawyer's office. She was there filing for alimony and child support. She never got either because Captain Barrow was "an Officer and a Gentleman" and outranked Judge Gerdine. I was there when my father, the "officer and the gentleman," punched my mother so hard she landed face down in the rock garden, the one she had designed to border the pathway to the road. She lay there, motionless. I thought he'd killed her.

He left and never came back.

I was there when my father deserted my mother.

And here I was in Washington D.C., after an all-night ride from Massachusetts. My mother was seated behind me. I was dressed up like some kind of lady to influence the judge. I heard angry voices. All of my own anger and hurt boiled up inside me. That was just the way I had felt when the Sheriff knocked on my mother's door two days ago. He asked my name. I told him, Shirley Carter. Why was he asking? How did he know I was in Worcester? I lived in Yarmouth, Maine. I had been dropped here months ago, when I was pregnant with our second baby girl. I never wanted to be here. Who was this uniformed man? Why was he asking about me? He simply said, "You are served" and left.

I had to show up in court within forty-eight hours or the divorce would have been awarded, uncontested, to my husband.

I bet my mother had a smirk on her face. She predicted this. She wished for this. She hated Oscar! She had wished my unborn child dead. I hated her for that. I had already lost a baby, a baby who died inside me at three months. The baby that doctors advised me to carry until nature expelled it as a foreign body. Why did I have to carry a dead baby?

"Your uterus is highly vascular at this time. If we did a D & C (dilation & curettage), you'd likely bleed to death." Nature's hemorrhage "removed" the foreign

63

body at four months going on five. I refused blood transfusions. My nursing experience biased me. I'd seen too many errors dealing with blood: wrong types, wrong factors, dire results.

Then I became pregnant again and, at three months, ended up at my mother's house, deposited by my husband who left me there with our young daughter. Why was I the one being sued for divorce now? I did not desert my husband! At the judge's last shout, my lawyer whispered in my ear, "We are going to change your plea...we are not going to contest this lie, we are going to countersue! The guy's a bastard." My lawyer had read the affidavit that Lee, my landlady in Maine, had faxed overnight. He spoke aloud to the judge, changing my plea from Contest to Countersue.

Lee, in her affidavit, recounted the hell day in Maine: the day I came home from a bus trip to Portland with our baby girl, Laurie. Lee and I were both dumbfounded, watching the last U-Haul trailer-load headed to storage. Oscar, with help from boys at his school, had emptied our entire household! Shocked, Lee and I had no idea what was happening or why. It wasn't until the long stony silent ride to Worcester that Oscar spoke.

"I'm taking you and the baby to your mother's house. I've been accepted to Howard University and will finish my Ph.D. Today my boss awarded a sabbatical to a new guy—a guy I trained! I was promised a sabbatical leave with half salary. They promised me last year! They said I'd have to go to Orono, to the University of Maine. They felt I'd never return and work my two years as agreed. Because I was accepted to Howard, they denied me. Well, I showed them. I resigned forthwith!"

My mother's house? Dear God, No! Please, no, I did not belong there. I fled that house as soon as I got my job in D.C.

"Did you call her?" I asked.

"No," he said.

We simply arrived, after dark.

Before the Sheriff knocked on the door to deliver my summons to the D.C. court, the baby had been born alive and healthy. Big sister Laurie had had her third birthday and had been in counseling at the Child Guidance Clinic for most of that time. Her grief at the loss of her Daddy caused her to cry inconsolably until she vomited. My mother concluded she had a devil in her. "She is just like her father. What are all these tears about? He's no good."

But now I was back in my body, here in a courtroom full of strangers, an angry judge, an absent husband and my mother, sitting behind me as witness to the fact that I did not desert my husband. Me, divorced. I had married for life! There was some mistake here. We could fix this.

At the last slam of the gavel, I heard, "Where's the Plaintiff?!"

Richard Cook raised his hands as if in praise. "I don't know, Your Honor; he was here just a minute ago."

"Out of prejudice, I award the divorce to counter claimant." Or some such strange word. Richard, stunned, raised his hand and asked the judge, "What about custody of the children?"

"They are wards of the state of Massachusetts: not germane to this case. Next!"

It was over. I was a divorced woman.

Oscar had fled the courtroom when I entered. I never saw him. It was years before he saw his children. Like my mother and at her insistence, I appealed to the court for child support, but he moved from state to state: D.C. to Virginia to Maryland. I gave up. During the following years, I felt like "damaged goods." In the early 1960s, divorced women were still not welcome in the Episcopal Church. In the 1930s, my mother had been asked to leave All Saints Church after my father left. We, his children, were welcome as long as we were able to pledge something to the church. We attended for a while when we were in grade school and then gave up attending church. That was an early confirmation to a young child of color that I was not desirable. I didn't lose God, and I even went to the Bishop in Springfield in order to marry. Oscar, a Southern Baptist, converted to the Episcopacy in order to marry me in church. Oscar certainly convinced me that I was very desirable.

I was not a young bride. At twenty-five, I found love, had a professional career, became a wife, a happy homemaker, then a mother. How naïve was I? We took vows. Even as I stood in the courtroom, I loved this man! Now I saw myself as damaged, as a woman unable to please or hold onto her man. A divorced woman! I never stopped loving him. Years later, he must have appreciated that I never maligned him to his daughters. I didn't have to. They felt the sting of desertion. They met his next wife and stayed briefly one summer with him and his next set of children. Bernard, his son, was very close in age to my baby girl.

In a desperate attempt to get out of my mother's house, I applied for housing in a project in Worcester. I was put on a waiting list. They allowed one black family per unit and one divorced person per building. The wait was worth it. We spent happy years in Great Brook Valley Gardens.

Was I damaged goods, single parent, woman of color, not woman enough to keep her man? No! I was and am a "late bloomer." It took years of reflection to accept that I was not like my mother. My fear at the time of the unwanted divorce was that I would become like her: bitter, unforgiving, judgmental. Yet both of her husbands stayed close to her until her death. Bill, her first husband, sent unsigned birthday cards every year, and my father was on the phone with her almost daily when she was confined to bed with terminal cancer.

The dutiful daughter became the dutiful wife. I never spoke up when my world began crashing apart. There was the angry judge who never looked at or recognized me, and the husband, a no-show. In my youth, there had been an angry father and a passive mother. My relationship with my husband was strikingly passive. Standing in that courtroom, I became that confused, frightened child. Sexism was also a culprit: I allowed my lawyer to speak for me, to request something I did not want. I had allowed my husband to make and expedite decisions I not only did not agree with but never confronted.

I knew how to throw a hissy fit! I could have refused to get in the car when my husband bid me. All hell could have broken loose that day in Maine. My ideas about marriage were rigid, influenced by church programming. I've threatened people's lives over lesser things. I could have said, "Worcester? Hell, no! I'm going with you. Wherever you go, I go!" It never occurred to me on that hellish day to say, "Are you out of your mind? You know my mother. You didn't even call her! Think again. We are going to Plan B, and it ain't Worcester!"

That's who I am today: a woman of conviction who speaks her mind. Amen.

CHAPTER 13

Friends and Neighbors

My first friends were our neighbors, the Milletts and the Wellwoods. I grew up with three generations of this family that made their access driveway off Ellen Street, where I lived. The eldest Milletts came from Maine. Herbert and Ella were the next generation, and they bought and built homes on Margin Street. Mr. and Mrs. Herbert Millett lived in a single house with their daughter, Sue, and her husband, Russell Wellwood, and their three children, Dottie, Gail and David. Sue's brother, Bob, lived next door. He married Hilvi, one of the Ingve girls from the neighborhood, and they had four children, Bobby, Eleanor, Frances and Patty. All of the young people on the street called the older couple Grampuh and Grammy Millett.

There was a little cottage that the Milletts owned and rented out. Bertha Birtz and her son, Bobby, lived there for many years. These children were my gang. Dottie Wellwood, Bobby and Eleanor Millett, and Bobby Birtz were close to my age. We learned together, played cooperative games like hide and seek, kick the can, hopscotch, snap-the-whip, jump rope and snappers. Snappers was a marble game requiring dexterity and skill. Jacks was another small ball toss game to collect jacks. We competed on sleds, crashing into each other, forcing the competitor into a snowbank. I did better with the gross motor skills like climbing trees and steering my sled, and I also often played dolls on Hilvi's front porch with the younger kids. They did not tease me about playing with dolls. Children respected my limited skills. Football, pig pile and green apple wars could earn you a bunch of bruises. The football game was non-traditional. Someone held the ball so one of the boys could kick it; there was a rush to catch it, and then you ran! You had to watch not to trip over the iron stakes used by the adults' horseshoe game. Pig pile began with a spontaneous call, usually by one of the big kids: "Pig pile!" Then everyone stopped whatever they were doing to jump on top of each other, making a human pile. You never wanted to be on the bottom, and everyone had a good laugh. I never participated in green apple wars for very long. I would gather my ammunition, filling my shirt and every pocket with firm, tiny green apples. I found good spots to duck behind when the first whizzing apples began to fly, but as soon as I dared to stand and fire my ammunition, an apple would smack me on the head or some other tender spot. It took only one knot on my head, and I would go home. Gentle games included everyone. We built roads, bridges and tunnels and drove small cars across Grampuh's huge garden plot before he plowed in the spring.

I enjoyed being one of the gang and still appreciate growing up in a time when every adult acted like a parent. They looked out for you and did not hesitate to chide you if need be. The Milletts' Uncle Harvey took reams of film of us children at play. As young adults, we viewed them again and could not help but laugh at our raggedy, grubby, happy selves. Children in that time wore play clothes after school, and we never worried about getting dirty. Dottie and David, the Wellwood children, are still my close friends. We get together and look back on those days with joy. Frances is the only Millet neighbor-child still living. We do not see each other often, yet we remain friends.

My first new neighborhood as an adult was in Georgetown, in Washington D.C. I lived at 2727 P Street in a one-room efficiency rental apartment with the Carter Bowman family. I did not build a lasting friendship with the family, but I know they viewed me as a responsible adult. I met folks in the neighborhood as I walked to work or to church. It was a friendly, safe neighborhood.

I lived another brief six months in D.C. at my future brother-in-law's apartment. I did not make friends in this neighborhood. It was a black neighborhood with a "rip off" corner store and frowning pedestrians. Scary. What I enjoyed was the evening ritual the neighbors followed on hot, muggy evenings. No one had air conditioning, and it was suffocating indoors. A small group would begin singing as they strolled around the block. The numbers would grow until the harmonies filled the night air. It turned a sticky, restless night into a pleasant, waking dream.

In the apartment, I was deemed trustworthy and a desirable female. That was confirmed when Ted, the future brother-in-law, loaned me his car. No other family member had earned that privilege. The brothers also confirmed my desirability when I became Mrs. Oscar D. Carter.

My next neighborhoods were in Portland and

Yarmouth, Maine. I made great friends at work, and my next-door neighbor in Portland became a best friend and confidante. She was elderly and alone, and I was a young wife and mother. We had long conversations in the common laundry room and many cups of tea at her kitchen table. I knew I had become a trusted good friend when she confided in me about what to do if there were a fire or if she died in her sleep. "Shirley, go in my refrigerator and take the mayonnaise jar. I don't believe in banks and some careless person might just toss it out!"

My landlady, Lee, and I became good friends when I moved to Yarmouth. She had twin daughters. We had similar parenting skills and entrusted each other with the children. The twins were school-aged yet looked out for my baby girl, Laura, who had just learned to walk. Lee loaned me her car so I could take all three girls to the lake. When my marriage crashed, she wrote an affidavit for the court describing and confirming the sudden disastrous events.

That is when my life came full circle. In August of 1959, when my husband summarily moved us out of our apartment in Yarmouth and left me and my daughter at my mother's house in Worcester, I was newly pregnant. He came back briefly when the new baby arrived and then never returned as my husband again. He had been my closest friend for nearly five amazing years. I learned that life can be fickle and wondered if love ever survives.

Returning to Worcester allowed me to reconnect with neighbors and classmates I consider true friends. I managed to escape from my mother's house by moving to the Garden Apartments at Great Brook Valley, a

72

housing project in north Worcester. It was a wonderful, close neighborhood in the early 1960's. I made lasting friendships with several families. The Beg family became parent allies, helping with transportation to our shared day care when I returned to work at Worcester City Hospital. I have remained close to some of those families for three generations, especially the Sullivans and the Nagles. Virginia McAvey lived there, too; we had known each other since Roosevelt Elementary School. The Great Brook Valley Gardens friendships were very special. I became a respected independent woman, full-time parent and wage worker.

CHAPTER 14

The Sisterhood

The bond that links your true family is not one of blood, but of respect and joy in each other's life...
—Richard Bach

Our friends tend to give us a peek at the self we know the least about. My family had stark ways of informing me of my shortcomings, thereby giving me a clear view of my less gifted side. My neighbor, Grampa Millett, even had difficulty knowing which Barrow girl I was. He'd say, "You're like Ike and Mike, you look alike." When that no longer entertained him, he'd call me "girl." Other folks in the neighborhood were a lot like him. They'd say, "Oh, you're one of the Barrow twins." My sister Audrey and I are not twins, yet for a month every year we are the same age. It was entertaining to us, too, that folks thought we were twins. We played along.

Over time, I became quite certain I wasn't Topsie or Stepin Fetchit, and I also knew I was quite indistinguishable: neither a monster nor a model. My mother often told me I was "her baby with two faces." After the baby fuzz rubbed off, the hair did not grow on the back of my head for a long time. It never did grow long. My baby pictures were lost in storage during the

Depression, but I could imagine what an infant looked like with a half-bald, wrinkled head. I made myself acceptable by being "good," whatever that might mean. With all of the name calling, grammar school was not a place to make friends, but I had many friends in middle school. I never considered running for class officer, but the whole idea of being a friend and helping with campaigning was an adventure. I'm proud to say I remain friends with several of those junior high classmates. There were few opportunities for friendships in high school. I was much too busy: commuting, studying and working. Dating never happened. I was not the right color. Still, I was satisfied being the good daughter, the good student and the good worker.

In adulthood, friendships came easily, and I added good friends to my list. Of the thirty-three women in my nursing class at Worcester City Hospital in the early 1950s, six of us have remained sisters through these many decades. Our class had male students, but the social standards of the times required that they live in apartments. All women lived in supervised dormitories: either Thayer Hall or the Memorial Home. The nursing school rules were very strict, not unlike a convent. I learned a great deal about myself during those three years living in Thayer Hall. My "family" grew. A group of us became very close, and I found I was both quite daring and a good organizer.

Madelyn and I were pranksters and committed several tricks that resulted in administrative investigations. We were never caught and kept most of our mischief completely secret. Toilet papering the medical doctors' dining hall got more attention than we anticipated. Other adventures, like decorating a cake box with a bloody placenta inside, a birthday ruse for an intern, were too shocking or perhaps too embarrassing to report. (Poor George, the intern, had a ravenous appetite and a well-known sweet tooth.)

In Thayer Hall, I became very adept at running across the roof in my pajamas to visit with classmates. We were not allowed to cross the first floor lobby in nightclothes, but the windows of the inner rooms on the second floor opened onto a roof: the ceiling of the central auditorium. It required a bit of upper body strength to hoist oneself out, but I had it in abundance at that time. As freshmen entered, upperclassmen moved one level up, so moving to the third floor brought an end to our roof crossing escapades.

Eloise Valerides, Madelyn Jasper, Ginny Sullivan, Claire Berard, Ethel Durkin, Jean Nargi and the Barrow sisters were members of the Cape Cod Crew. We had one week's vacation in summer, and six of us managed to barter or bargain for the same week. Ethyl and Jean only came once, but there was a core of six each year we lived in Thayer Hall. We rented a cabin on Bassett Lane in Hyannis and spent a riotous week together. I made all the arrangements, and the adventure was well-planned. Ginny's brother loaned us his automobile. There were conditions. Before our first trip, we were required to go to the Sullivans' house to learn how to change a flat tire and check the oil. Ginny's brother was a saint. The Sullivans lived way out of the city in the Brookfields. This was well before the days of two cars in a family, and he travelled to work by bus for a week!

It was a full two-hour ride to Hyannis. On our first trip, we found ourselves rolling along beside a convertible that carried a group of boys. They flirtatiously invited one of us girls to join them for a spin. As I recall, I was driving, and I laughed off the idea. Well, didn't Ginny hop out when we stopped at a light and join them! We kept up with each other for miles, and then Ginny hopped back into our car. It was the nineteen fifties, but even then I was very anxious, and we all scolded our daring friend. We committed to sticking together from then on. My mother had advised, "If anyone tries to give you trouble, hold hands and run!" We had an opportunity to heed her advice.

One evening, a rowdy crowd came wandering out of a bar as we were walking home to our cabin. It was dark. They were hooting, whistling and caterwauling as they advanced towards us. We looked at one another, and we did it: the six of us clasped hands and ran full out. Safety became our priority.

Most days we spent on the beach. We collected big conch shells, surprised to find them inhabited by large snails. We treated Madelyn's sunburn, did gymnastics on the lawn and cooked nourishing meals. We had company. One of the hospital orderlies knew we were headed for Hyannis, and he dropped by. He was a handsome young man and a bit full of himself. We decided to mess with him. We had boiled the conches to remove the snails and debated eating the meat. We decided against it, but that didn't mean we were going to throw it out. We chopped it finely with a bit of mayonnaise and onion and made Mr. Headinstead a "tuna fish" sandwich. He thanked us, and just as he was about finished, we told him it was snail. Out it flew from his mouth. He later admitted it actually tasted rather good.

Bassett Lane Cabins

We graduated in 1952 and soon became Mrs. Eloise Kujawski, Mrs. Madelyn Sheahan, Mrs. Genevieve Monast, Mrs. Claire Wasgatt, Mrs. Ethyl Duggan, Mrs. Jean Semonelli, Mrs. Audrey Brown and Mrs. Shirley Carter. The sisterhood continued. We looked out for our mothers, assisted by our sisters. We had children who knew each other from our annual outings at camps during the sixties. We attended the weddings of each other's children. Claire, Ethyl and Madelyn have left us, but those of us still here gather at our nursing school's annual reunion. We have wonderful memories. After we turned eighty, I, as the class's corresponding secretary, spent months locating as many of my sisters as possible so we could celebrate our graduation from the Worcester City Hospital School of Nursing sixty plus years ago. We have stuck together ever since our Thayer Hall days.

CHAPTER 15

Eliane Remax Nagle Landry Harrison

Eliane was all that. She was one of Marcelle Remax's daughters, born in France. The Remax family came to the United States when Eliane was a teenager. Ellie and I met in the Project, in Great Brook Valley. We lived way off the road in the Garden Apartments, bordering large grassy fields. The units were two-story apartments with single story units for the elderly on each end. There was a back road, but to get the bus, we had to pass by the high-rise apartments off Lincoln Street. The Garden Apartments were beautiful. Cedar enclosures hid the clotheslines, and there were plots of land near each doorway where tenants planted flowers. My apartment fronted on a meadow full of wildflowers. I dabbled in watercolors and tried to capture them in my paintings.

I had been on public relief, receiving support from the State of Massachusetts to help feed my daughters. My divorce was fresh, and my former husband had put himself beyond reach of the courts. The Worcester Housing Authority was very strict in those years. I called it "social programming." They limited the number of single parents in a unit and, as a woman of color, I had to go on a waiting list in order to maintain a racial balance. Federal laws declared those rules illegal, and today the Project is more like a ghetto.

Eliane was a colorful character: her flamboyant femininity, French accent and love of dancing, cards, the beach and children made her special. She and I went to the playground to supervise our children as well as to events the Project held for families. She had three young ones: Michael, the oldest, was my older daughter's age, and her twins, Danny and Denise, were near in age to my younger girl. I was not part of the lively gang who went to Eliane's house with bags of pennies and played cards into the wee hours. Our connection was through our children. We went to the library and attended any inexpensive program for children. We worried about doing our best as single parents and laughed a lot about what our children were teaching us. I was strict about bedtime. Most children played outside after dark. My girls called me "the mean Mom." I bemoaned the sadness I felt to Eliane. But I stuck to my rules, and I learned not to feel so bad. One evening, my children were whining when I called them in. I was upstairs when I overheard them explaining to their playmates: "My mother cares about us and we go to bed early so we can do well in school. See ya tomorrow." I was pleased to discover that they understood my behavior. I added a few more good safety rules and remained a "mean Mom."

We moved out of the Valley's Garden Apartments in January of 1965. The world was changing rapidly, and my social worker had given me excellent advice:

"Now that you are working, they will raise your rent," she warned. "You will be trapped in the projects. Save your money, and before the new rents come out, find a small apartment in the city."

I shared the information with Eliane. She had begun a new job, waitressing. My rent was forty dollars a month. My part-time nursing job would increase my rent to four hundred dollars a month. We both moved. Our connection with children's activities ended.

I found an apartment in my old neighborhood, just three rooms, but I had the support of my family. My mother and Audrey lived within walking distance. My daughters went to the same grammar school I had attended and had some of the same teachers.

The conversations Ellie and I now had were about our love lives. Mine was full of doubt and questions. Eliane's was racy, complicated and full of angst.

"Shirley, what do you think I should do about Bill? His mother is sooo jealous of the time we spend together, and he won't leave her house! He's so goood to her. She is an invalid and he looks after her. That's a good sign, isn't it?"

There was always drama. Her French accent never left her. The French flair and her animation enhanced every story. Our children grew to adulthood and went off to school and to work. Eliane and I went camping and to the beach. We introduced each other to our friends and family. I met Ellie's mother, Marcelle, and we all went to the movies together. Nellie, Eliane's sister, lives on Cape Cod. I met many of her relatives from France and enjoyed days at the beach and on her brother-in-law's boat. We loved the beach. I swam. Eliane packed fancy picnic lunches with wine coolers and sat in the sun.

One summer day, she and I were at Revere Beach, near Boston, when a fierce rainstorm struck. It was windy with lightning and hail. We huddled inside my

Volkswagen camper. The parking lot was flooded. Darkness fell, and the lightning flashes over the ocean were breathtaking. The lot emptied, but we decided it was safer to stay overnight in the camper and go home in daylight. After we returned to Worcester the next day, we stopped by my house for breakfast. There were frantic messages on my answering machine. Both of our daughters demanded that we contact them as soon as possible!

"Where were you?" My daughter was chastising me! I could barely get a word in. Eliane's daughter was also righteously angry and frightened. "We had that terrible storm and you guys said you were going to the beach. Why didn't you call?" It was clear that they were more frightened than angry. We let them rant and once we apologized and finished the calls, we began to laugh. Our daughters had become our parents! We could hear our own scolding in their voices. It was before cell phones, but we did find better ways to keep in touch... for safety's sake.

It was some time after her fiftieth birthday that Ellie decided she was through with New England winters and moved to Florida. She chose Daytona Beach because she had a friend there. Her son, Michael, promised to share the driving and accompany her. They had a yard sale and packed her van. It made me sad to see her go, but with my good friend, Inés, also living in Florida, it gave me more reason to take my winter school breaks there.

The week that Ellie was to leave, Michael discovered that he could not get the time off. She expected it would take her two days to get to Daytona, and she was reluctant to go by herself.

"Ohhh, Shirleeey, is there any way possible that you could drive down with me?" she pleaded.

I was working full-time and on a new health kick to lose weight. Nutrisystem had come to Worcester. They opened a store on Park Avenue where one could get a computerized weight loss program, meet with a counselor and, of course, buy their food. They guaranteed weight loss. When Inés had moved to Miami Beach, I had worried every day while she drove from Worcester to Florida by herself. It took her two days and I insisted she call me each evening...for safety's sake. I could not refuse Eliane now.

I took time off from work, bought my weekly supply of Nutrisystem food and off we went. We had some silly, giggling incidents: no wine, just losing time trying to get off the Beltway in Washington, D.C. After dusk on the first day, we looked for an inexpensive motel that didn't have a row of parked cars with in-state plates, the telltale sign of one-night rendezvous. We were just past the Virginia border when we found a decent place. There was no manager in the office, but keys hung neatly on the wall. We walked about and shouted but found no one, so we took a set of keys and left a note. The next morning, the office was still empty. We looked at one another, grabbed our note with our names and license plate number and hurried out of there!

The rest of our drive was uneventful, and we entered Daytona Beach driving alongside the ocean. Eliane spotted a trailer park off the side of a lovely bridge. We went to her friend's house, where she planned to stay until she found a place of her own, and I left soon after to return home. My next visit to Daytona found Eliane living in the very trailer park she had seen coming into the city. On that trip, we spent some fantastic days on a beach where automobiles and dune buggies mingled with the bathers. Eliane's picnic lunches became low calorie but still delicious. She had convinced me that diets do not work.

"Shirley, they only want your monaayy!"

Eliane and Shirley

CHAPTER 16

Daytona Beach

Eliane enjoyed waitressing, and her tips in Florida were generous. Her genuine desire to please complemented her spunky personality. She brought laughter to any conversation and loved meeting people. We shared a common joy in simple things, like watching the sunset or spotting the first evening star. She was a devoted employee and a hard worker. If a workmate wanted time off, she would fill in for them. When the boss called looking for extra help, Ellie was pleased to be chosen and always went in.

She managed to buy a house and eventually a second-hand convertible automobile. She adored that car and drove like the wind. In response, I often pressed my feet against the floor and closed my eyes so that I couldn't distract her by gasping or screaming aloud. She must have picked up some kind of inspiration from the famous Daytona racetrack. She did not drive like that in Massachusetts!

Her long-term boyfriend, Will, owned a fancy motorcycle. They went on trips across the U.S. with groups of other bikers and toured Europe together. It was an acrimonious relationship, but difficult for her to let go of: her love affair extended to the bike. We wrote frequently and her many letters focused on her ambivalent feelings about Will. Each year, we set aside special-time to be together. We often included my friend, Inés, and Audrey joined some of our adventures. We visited secondhand boutiques and out-of-the-way charming lunchrooms—and of course, the beach! I went south in the winter, and she came north in the summer. Denise, her daughter, married twice, and the second husband brought her and her children to Florida. I could wake up any hot summer day and find Ellie on my front porch, waiting for me to get out of bed and head for the beach. Her daughter would sometimes be there, too, with a big picnic lunch, ready to "beat the traffic." One year during my school break, I had signed on for a weekend workshop and could not travel to Florida to join her. It broke my heart, but Ellie had a cheerful solution. She apologized for arriving unan-nounced in Worcester and asked if she could stay at my house while I attended the workshop. She was good at flexible planning and elegant solutions. Our compati-bility confounded Leo, the man I was dating. He enjoyed Ellie's company, and they would speak French, roaring with laughter. I had no clue what was so funny but was certain it was provocative. Leo was convinced Eliane and I had a lesbian relationship. "No women can be that close," he often said, "and she openly admits how much she loves you!" He later made the same com-ment about Inés when the three of us—Ellie, Inés and I—went camping together. I told them about his com-ment, and it entertained us to think men could not understand closeness that did not include sex. It seemed that society deprived men of developing close-ness with other men. It is actually quite sad.

I chose not to remarry, but Eliane found a new partner, Frank, who cherished her as much as she cherished him. I liked Frank, and her family liked him, too. I first met him at her sister Nellie's home in Chatham when Nellie hosted a lavish reception for them. I continued my winter visits to the home they shared in Florida. Our connection remained strong and deepened as I supported her through his sudden death and painful legal tangles with his adult children. They contested his will, which left everything to her, including the home where they had grown up. She generously gave them the house against her lawyer's advice, kept the resources he had left her and moved into a trailer near the beach.

Our conversations centered on our hopes and dreams, the things we longed to do but never found time to follow through with. Eliane committed to learning new things and traveling. Her education had ended in France when the family relocated. We both took courses at colleges near our homes. When she visited me, she sat in on the courses I was taking at Worcester State College. My course in Beginning French was especially enjoyable for her. My creative writing course inspired me to complete a published work. I loved writing and previously had written mostly journals. I traveled often during my years of singing with the college's chorale, and Ellie signed up with me to go on one of its biannual international trips, a ten-day trip to Greece. Planning together was exciting. Ellie would come to Worcester early in May to stay with me before we left.

It never happened.

Michael was the one who called me. "Mother is dead. The police found her early this morning, jammed against the trailer door."

I could hardly breathe as I asked him to repeat what I could not believe I had heard. His voice was flat, emotionless. He repeated the unthinkable and added:

"She didn't answer her phone last night, and I got worried. They won't let me come until they rule out foul play. Her robe was tangled around her neck, her coffee still warm on the kitchen table. There's nothing I can do until Forensics finishes their investigation. Denise is on her way, I just called Danny."

I was numb. I thought about the biker boyfriend who was back, romancing her again. He was the jealous type. I agonized until evening. While I waited, I dialed Eliane's phone number and left a loving message for her children; I was certain they would gather there. We were all somewhat relieved to learn she had died suddenly, with little or no pain, from an aortic aneurism.

Eliane on Motorcycle

I kept many of her letters. When I read them, I cannot help but smile. Eliane was such a good friend: funny, sexy, adventuresome and attractive. Yes, she was all that.

CHAPTER 17

Inés

I met Inés Eskenas de Rebeca at a folk dance in the early seventies. We discovered we had a great deal in common: we were parents, divorcees, dancers, nurses, lovers of the outdoors. We went camping, spent time with each other's families, traveled together. When we met, both of our mothers were still alive but failing in health. When they died, we supported each other even when geography separated us. Each February, I'd migrate to Inés' place in Florida, and come summer, we'd find a week to go camping in New England. We could, laugh, cry and play for days on end. She thought I was very special, and I had no doubt about how wonderful she was. We kept every letter we'd written to each other.

Our friendship swelled naturally, like orzo in chicken soup. The day we met, we left the dance group and had lunch at her apartment on Providence Street; that was my introduction to orzo and its amazing capacity to fill the soup pot. Inés introduced me to her granddaughters. After another adventure at line dancing, she came along with me on an errand I had promised to do for my mother, and we spent the evening at Ma's house. My mother liked Inés. They were easy together, never at a loss for conversation and laughter. It was not always easy to enjoy my mother, and to hear her laugh allowed me to remember happier times. Old age confused her. She believed she had a right to make demands. She would ask for constant attention and for assistance, meeting basic needs she could easily manage herself: "Get me my slippers. Well, don't just stand there, put them on my feet!" It became challenging for her adult daughters not to resent this "the world owes me a living" attitude. As her younger daughter, I found myself still attempting to please her. That had been my role as a young one. Even then, I knew no one could ever meet her needs.

Inés and I nurtured each other in so many ways. We shared our best thinking. We talked endlessly about parenting skills, how to cope with aging parents, our professional challenges, our divorces and how that rupture affected our children. She would look at me or at a photograph of me and remind me that I was a beautiful woman. I was not aware of that truth. I considered Audrey to be "the pretty one." She had the long curls with the red and blond streaks. There were so many truths about me that Inés pointed out. Now I can look at pictures of myself and see that I was an adorable little girl and grew into a beautiful woman. It is a bit sad that my friend's observation was the first time I could see the beauty.

Inés and I had been friends for over twenty years before she decided to move to Miami Beach. She wanted to be near Rebeca, her mother, and later she took a job at sea, serving as pharmacist on a National Oceanic and Atmospheric Administration (NOAA) ship, the *Researcher*. Before she left, giving away everything that would not fit into her old jalopy for the drive to Florida,

Inés got to meet Eliane, my old neighbor and friend from the Great Brook Valley housing project. By the time I introduced them, Ellie and I had long since raised our children, moved away from the Valley and found decent jobs. She, like Inés, had lots of energy and loved camping. We became a mutual admiration society, getting together regularly to go camping, just us women. On one of those adventures in my secondhand Volkswagen camper, we explored the tip of Cape Cod. We drove out to an old lighthouse. It was unoccupied but well maintained. We spread out our lunch on the sandy, shady slope and watched the boats out at sea. It was beautiful, completely relaxing. I do not remember our even having a lot to say. When the sun began to sink on the horizon, we brushed ourselves off, left the rocky, gull-adorned seascape and headed for the camper. We had parked facing the shore, but now the camper sat like an island, perched on the only bit of road not covered by the incoming tide. It (and we) had been marooned! After a few ghastly moments, we realized that in fact the tide was already reversing. We did not have a camera, but it was truly a Kodak moment to watch Eliane, cautious not to spoil her hairdo or make-up, dog paddling in the road toward the van. Inés and I tested the bottom. The water was only waist high and warm as bath water. We breast stroked halfway down the road, splashing and laughing our heads off. A wee bit sunburned and completely pleased with our lunacy, we drove back to the campground in Truro.

CHAPTER 18

Jogging, Junkets & Just Plain Fun

Well before computers were in every home and library, Inés found sources for inexpensive trips. We were both working, and I was still in my fifties when she researched and organized a trip to Alaska. Audrey and I had already been there on a Collette guided tour. I had fallen in love with the people and the place and did not hesitate to return. When Audrey learned of our plan, she came along with us.

This inexpensive trip was aboard a cargo ship that would travel the coastal waterways, delivering supplies. It was October, the last run it would make for the year. Snow and serious winter storms would begin before the end of the month. Indigenous Alaskans rode free. Travelers could bring pets, pitch tents on deck or rent an inexpensive four-person cabin.

We rented a cabin yet spent very little time there. I was fascinated watching the loading of huge tandem trailer trucks, panel trucks and heavy machinery. If the tides were right, we could go ashore for the few hours it took to load up. We all enjoyed those layovers. We visited the shops for end-of-the-season bargains and chatted with town folks and artisans. There were times when we could buy tasty treats. I saved the day on one of these shore excursions.

We had finished our lunch and were having one of those wonderful unexpected conversations with the shopkeeper. She was closing down the kitchen for the winter, flying to Hawaii on the weekend. She spent every winter there and found it reasonable. My sister and I chimed in, "Our brother, Herbert, lives there on the Big Island." The conversation became very animated. She went on to explain, "Profits from the shop plus my oil dividend make it possible for me to vacation for the entire season!" We were curious about the "oil dividend." That is when we heard it: the ship whistle's blasting the all-aboard call. Inés cried out, "Oh, no! If we don't get on board, we're stuck here, no place to stay, nothing until the ship goes back down to Seattle. Run!" We ran, waving our arms. We were close enough to see them hauling up the gangplank. I led the pack. I had been a proud jogger—a few years back. I outdid myself. They couldn't finish hauling in the gangplank because I stood on it until Inés and Audrey caught up. We were lucky.

The rest of the trip was pure fun. I was awake each night past midnight reading James Michener's *Alaska* from cover to cover. Audrey was up until the wee hours, playing card games with the Athabaskans. Inés was up at dawn practicing Tai Chi, aft of the ship. She spent most of the daytime petting and walking dogs and befriending their owners, most of whom slept in the tents. I'm not sure what a vagabond is, but that's what it felt like, wandering around aboard ship and on shore, as long as the tide allowed.

On another junket, Inés and I rode the trains across country. She found tickets that allowed passengers to get on and off at will. We boarded near Brownsville

Junction in Maine, crossed Canada and then went down to Wisconsin. Our trip began at a bed & breakfast in Bar Harbor. It was a grand old house with a wide staircase, mirrors, lace curtains and ruffles everywhere. There was no television, no phone in the room, a clawfoot bathtub and a porcelain pull chain on the toilet. It was simple, elegant and cheap! The house was located right on the street near the specialty shops. Bar Harbor is a vacation beach town, and we spotted a shop that invited tourists to dress up in old-fashioned clothes and have their photograph taken. Why not? It took a bit of time, but the price was right.

The next shop that caught my attention was the bike rental shop.

"Hey, Inés, we can explore this lovely place on bikes."

Inés was usually game for all adventure, but now she was vigorously shaking her head. She read the surprise on my face and explained, "I've never been on a bike in my life!" The shopkeeper took in our conversation and came up with an elegant solution, once more at an irresistible price.

"We have tandems," he said to me. "Your friend can sit on the back, peddle if she likes or just sit. They are easy to handle, and this is a pedestrian-bicycle plaza. No traffic, no worries! Come on, ladies, I'll help you."

He did. Inés gripped the handlebars, set her jaw and off we went. I peddled all around the plaza, past the bed & breakfast, over hill and dale with Inés squealing and giggling at every turn. Radiant at the end of our junket, she convinced the shopkeeper to take our picture before she got off the bike.

"My family won't believe it unless they see it!"

Inés & Shirley on Tandem Bicycle

Bar Harbor was a great start for our three-day journey. We left our automobile at Inés' niece's home and took a cab to Brownsville Junction, where we would board the Canadian train. When the cabby loaded our bags into the trunk, we noticed a tiny cylinder of propane gas. We gasped.

"This is the cab's fuel?"

"If I can't get it filled, the engine can run on gasoline, too," he assured us.

97

The next two nights, we slept on the train, getting off in Toronto for a day. We enjoyed dinner and had cranberry pie for dessert. It was delicious. Gawking out the train window consumed the daylight hours, and our journey ended in Milwaukee, Wisconsin. My daughter and her family lived there. We visited with them and wandered through the many parks and neighborhood pubs. An ethnic restaurant caught Inés' eye. She saw a soup on their menu, a soup her mother used to make. She spoke to the waiter in Arabic, confirming the ingredients. He was thrilled to respond in Arabic and showered us with attention. It was lemon soup, an interesting culinary adventure. One could never travel with Inés, a petite, Sephardic Jew with snow white hair who spoke Ladino, Arabic and a wee bit of Turkish, without having fun!

CHAPTER 19

Deep Water Harbor

It was not unusual to receive a call from Inés in the middle of the night.

"Shirley! I need a nurse consultation. I've got a seaman here with acute angina. He's stable and doesn't want to leave the ship. In an hour, we'll be too far for a med flight. What do you think?"

I'd ask for details, the medical history and her worst-case scenario. We'd literally decide the sailor's fate together. I could roll over, go back to sleep and know I would eventually learn the outcome. We'd never worked together, but she knew I was a very good nurse as well as a very good friend. In contrast, my sister, who is also a nurse, was once working a unit where there was an urgent need for extra help. I was working part-time in the same hospital, and the supervisor suggested I work Audrey's unit when I came on duty. Audrey said, "I've never worked with her. Never mind sending me a nurse, give me two good aides. You can afford to pay them overtime." She named the aides she wanted!

The National Oceanic and Atmospheric Administration (NOAA) routinely docks their ships for maintenance. Inés used these extended layovers as opportunities. She could be involved with other work or just vacationing. When her ship, the *Researcher*, was in Miami Beach Harbor, she worked in the Cuban Clinic. The ship was lying over one February when I came to visit. Often, because I was on vacation from teaching school, she would block out some vacation days herself. It was always a pleasure to leave New England mid-winter and spend time at the beach! When Inés came home from work, we would head for the ocean. It was never crowded after five in the evening, and the sun was low in the sky. We could relax, swim, walk and even nap. If she was not working and we went to the beach after breakfast, Inés could not relax after the first hour. "Shirley, it's ten o'clock, we have to get off the beach. The rays are too strong! We can come back after four." If I dared to doze off, even under our umbrella, she would rap on my body to accentuate the urgency.

One day, it was my pleasure to spend an afternoon with her at the Cuban Clinic.

She handed me a lab coat. "Here, put this on and just follow me wherever I go."

That was not an easy thing to do. No one spoke English. All conversations were loud and rapid, patients sat in every room and staff members zoomed around as if they were on roller skates. Between doing intakes and treating patients, everyone sipped tiny paper souffle cups of sweet, strong, Cuban coffee. I am sure keeping up with Inés was one cause of my heart palpitations, but it was clear to me that it was also that one tiny cup of coffee. We had more than enough energy to spend long hours at the beach.

The *Researcher* could only dock for maintenance in deep water harbors. Inés would call me from many ports around the globe. One call came from Djibouti,

Africa. To make a call, one had to ask for a turn using the ship to shore service, which required each caller to use the term "over" when it was their turn to speak!

The most memorable of her calls came from Barbados.

"We will be here for a few more weeks," she told me. "I found a cheap weekend package for you: round trip flight and hotel. You will be just a bus ride away, and we can spend each day together. There are only a few of us aboard ship, and my light duty gives me every afternoon and evening free. I will cover all our meals, and you can get a good tour of the ship. What do you say? Can you swing it?"

It was an opportunity that comes but once. My paternal great-grandfather and at least three uncles were born in Barbados. I did not hesitate. I have no recall of what it cost. I managed it.

Barbados is postcard beautiful: lush flora and fauna, banana trees in courtyards, pastel cottages on stilts, tiny shops with board planks covering the cement gullies in front. I took a cab to my hotel. It was within walking distance to the beach, so I spent time there before settling in for the night. Inés called before I went to sleep. She gave me all the bus details and described our best meeting place for the next day. I nearly missed the bus. I was standing on the wrong side of the road!

The ride to town revealed the shanties: thatched roofs and houses on spindly stilts sheltering brightly dressed folks with smiling brown faces. The curious wood planks in front of the shops soon lost their mystery. We had a rain shower that caused all the roads to flood, and umbrellas were of little use. I got soaked. The gullies in front of the shops filled and gushed like rivers. Then the sun popped out, the balmy winds blew, the sidewalks quickly dried and so did I.

Inés and I had our meals together, and I toured the ship. Her shared quarters were tiny. Each had a bunk and small cubbies for personal belongings. I had to duck through doorways, step over each threshold and hang on tightly going down narrow, winding metal stairs. A ship is not a suitable place for a claustrophobic.

I did some research before my visit ended. I found the Marshall Farm that my uncle's brother still owned and visited the Episcopal church. There were many people and places with my maiden name, Barrow. Inés and I spent our last day together down near the dock at the deep water harbor. Artisans lined the walkways, demonstrating their crafts. I bought two pair of hand-crafted earrings made of abalone and polished black rock. I was sure my daughters would love them. They did not. One said, "I couldn't wear these, they are too art deco. Not in fashion. I could use one as a lapel pin." The younger one bluntly said, "Gosh, Mom, _you_ must have liked them; why don't you keep them? I can't wear them." Indeed, I do love them, not just because they are handmade and beautiful, but because they always remind me of my dear friend, Inés, and the deep water harbor in Barbados. My friendship with Inés gave me opportunities not only to learn about myself but also to visit places I'd only heard about from family members. I speak of Inés in the past tense. Indeed, it was a wonderful lifetime we shared.

June 20, 2000

The windows opened, and the zeros made the tunnel space just right. Zoom. She glided right through the centers, never bumping the edges. Inés flew home to her mother, Rebeca, and her beloved brother, Victor. They were waiting.

My first notice of my friend's leaving was the call from her sister, Ruthie.

"My sister passed," she told me. "They may have a service on Tuesday. I'd like to go down. I'll need a wheelchair and oxygen, but US Air doesn't do that. My daughter is calling Delta."

Inés Eskenas de Rebeca was dead.

I attempted to keep my shock, grief and disappointment in check. No one had informed me about Inés' final, failing health event so that I could have been at her side.

"It's a bit overdue..." her son, Brian, said when he called later to inform me. I was not ready.

Brian continued to explain, "She's had two recent hospital admissions, a coma and hospice care."

Another call came from Linda, her niece from New York.

"Brian didn't want to tell too many people," she said.

This disturbed me. I had been to see Inés when she had been in rehab and aphasic after her stroke. The staff was amazed that she had called out my name. I had come to know many of her family members, and they all knew me. How was it that none of them had thought to call me until she had died?

"Brian's wife doesn't even know," Linda said. "She's traveling. I know he tried to call you. I'm going down with them on Tuesday. Zachary gave me your number."

103

She prattled on, amazed that Zach, the younger grandson, had remembered my phone number. It reminded her of the family legend about Zach's older brother, Sam, who had inherited his Grandma Inés' gift of healing.

I knew about the boys. Zach, as a baby, had supposedly traveled the zeros and returned to life when Inés held him. The first time it happened, Sam was the one who woke Inés to tell her his mother was crying, and his baby brother wasn't breathing. When Inés picked Zach up, he came back to life. SIDS was never confirmed, but there were several more events of apnea. Each time the baby stopped breathing, Sam was the one to notice and find his grandma. Together, they beckoned him back to life. With his gift of alertness and his faith in Grandma, Sam was deemed as talented in healing as Inés. My friend was indeed a healer, and she had many admirers in addition to her extended family.

Linda, of course, knew the story well, but I didn't understand why she was talking about it now.

They gathered in Florida without me.

We all depart. Inés had had her travel notice when she began falling, when the strokes left permanent damage, when the water on the brain required surgery or she'd not only lose control of her balance and bladder, but her breathing, too. She had decided then not to use her exit ticket: she held onto it and approved risky brain surgery.

"I want my grandchildren and great-grandchildren to see and to know old people can survive. This surgery could repair my brain. What do you think, Shirley? I think I'm going to let them do it, for the children."

She did. She triumphed. I have photos of Inés wrapped in a bright, colorful afghan, half her head shaved, beaming at the camera. Inés' path was always chosen along a way where others could benefit. Her spunky, adventurous nature allowed her to enjoy many lifelong friendships: Maria, Jill, Ike and me, along with many whom I did not meet. Her generosity included sharing love with all who were fortunate enough to know her.

She moved to Miami Beach to be near Rebeca, then went to sea on the NOAA ship, the Researcher. Her mother had still been alive when the NOAA Ship's Pharmacist job opportunity came up. Rebeca was nearing her one hundredth birthday. She was frail, yet still living independently with family assistance. It was in Rebeca's apartment that I met Victor. He was playing the piano, and Inés, Rebeca and I were singing with him. This new job opportunity was unique. Inés would be the first woman in NOAA history to be hired in this position. She would be out to sea for months at a time. It worried her that she would be away from her aging mother for long periods. Inés was the most diligent visitor of all Rebeca's children.

"But Momma, what if you should become ill and die?" she asked. "I may be too far away to come to you."

With the loving, reassuring smile mothers know how to beam, Rebeca bid her, "Go! This is an opportunity for you. You can't stop me from dying."

And go she did, many times, around the world.

Our Mothers

Rebecca Eskenas

Dorothy Barrow

CHAPTER 20

The Beginning

The two most important days in your life are the day you were born and the day you found out why.

—Mark Twain

The writing journey I am on is fleshed with reminiscence as I continue to discover how I came to know who I am. Too often, we spend major portions of our early lives trying to be who or what those around us expect or want us to be. I was the dutiful daughter. The price I paid for that effort left me a tad bankrupt: with nothing left to spend on discovering all that I *could* be.

I was the quiet, cautious child whom no one had to worry about. It was my investment in myself in order to prevent my mother and other adult relatives from breaking my spirit. Breaking a child's spirit was the often-expressed goal they set for dealing with my sister. She was not dutiful.

We are, indeed, born with a certain disposition or nature. My sister was destined to be a manager, type A, top sergeant kind of person. She has no use for diplomacy, no need for finesse. She chose a path that frequently collided with my mother's expectations. Fortunately, the adults never accomplished their goal. Whipping, binding, blindfolding, being forced to eat regurgitated food, rattaning[3]: all of these as well as other horrendous attempts failed to break her spirit. Yet they were very successful in solidifying my own decision to be the "good" daughter. I was always treated well and, perhaps as a result, developed a rich, creative inner world of dreams and goals. I knew I had gifts.

Perhaps they came from the cosmos. I once found it entertaining to see what was in the stars, and I "Googled" my birthdate. I was born under the astrological sign of Scorpio, conceived on or about the second of February of 1931. It was a Monday. I left my mother's womb on October 26, 1931 in the Chinese Year of the Goat. It was eleven months after my sister was born, both of us Scorpios, both born on a Monday. The old English nursery rhyme says "Monday's child is fair of face, Tuesday's child is full of grace, Wednesday's child was full of woe, Thursday's child has far to go, Friday's child is loving and giving, Saturday's child works hard for a living, and the child born on the Sabbath Day is bonny and blithe, and good and gay." The rhymes were sung or recited so that children would learn the days of the week and discover their destiny. It seems people have been concerned with all manner of signs to predict a child's disposition.

Scorpio's strength keywords are loyal, passionate, resourceful, observant and dynamic, but also weakness, jealous, obsessive, suspicious, manipulative and unyielding. In the protracted list of characteristics, we are said to be fiercely independent.

---

[3] Rattaning was a form of corporal punishment, used in school, whereas a child's hands were hit with a ruler or wooden rod, on the palms for girls, knuckles for boys.

My numerology index, known as my Life Path Number, is five. Established by a child's date of birth, this number represents who she is at birth and the native traits that will carry her through life. Destiny is at work even before we are born! My number, five, claims I entered this earthly plane with a highly progressive mindset, with the attitudes and skills to make the world a better place. The key word for my Life Path is freedom. The numerology index goes on and on, but I stopped looking for further proof of my suspected innate gifts. With all of this Google information, how could I not be pleased by who I have become?

CHAPTER 21

Marie, aka Mimi

Some friendships develop after periods of acrimony. My first contact with Marie was awkward due to her preconceptions. There are people one hears about and has no interest in meeting. Befriending this woman was unimaginable.

We met at an engagement party hosted by my younger daughter and her espoused, Walter Joseph Reis, Junior. He was one of Marie's four cherished children, Michael, Anne Marie, Walter and Yvonne.

The wedding announcement made Marie vociferously unhappy, and she made her displeasure known, loud and clear. Her husband, Walter Senior, was more discreet, yet he later supported his wife when she told their son, "Walter, that Mary of yours is not welcome at Grandmother Reis's funeral. You know your grandmother strongly disapproved of you marrying that black girl!"

It was years ago when Marie was vehemently convinced her gentle son, Walter, had wantonly disgraced their entire family. Her son, Michael, and daughter, Anne Marie, had already married. Their partners were practicing Roman Catholics, of similar heritage and social class. Their mother and father, one of Irish heritage and the other Portuguese, were proud of those children. There were no grandchildren, and none on the way. Yvonne, a young adult at the time, was confused by her mother's disrespect and displeasure toward Walter's fiancée. She supported him and his choice of bride, though she was a bit competitive, wanting the lion's share of her brother's attention.

Mary was ambivalent about inviting Marie and Walter Senior to the engagement party. They lived in Marlborough, not far from Mary's Boston apartment, where the event was to take place. It could be inviting disaster to an evening meant to be a joyful celebration. After long consideration with young Walter, me and her Aunt Lois, my half-sister, Mary extended the invitation to Walter's parents. The most logical and expected outcome was for them to send their regrets. Why would Marie show up and allow her racist stance to be exposed publicly?

Young Walter had already decided his mother's opinion would not influence his choice of wife. He and Mary had met at university. His love and admiration for her continued to grow after Mary graduated. He met Mary's friends and a host of relatives and was ready to forsake his family to join hers.

Mr. and Mrs. Reis did show up, though a bit late. Marie sat on the edge of a chair, making contentious inquiries of those seated near her.

"Oh, so you are both nurses?" She looked incredulously at my sister, Audrey, and then announced, "My Walter is at university, training to be a professional nurse."

My sister, Lois, was interrogated as to how she was related and what she did for a living. The questioning continued throughout the evening.

Mary had lived with Lois in Boston while she attended school. My daughter transferred to a different university, and after a junket across Europe and a job in London, she graduated and now had a job that allowed her to rent this lovely apartment in Back Bay, the South End of Boston. Gentrification of the area had just begun. Lois was a Clinical Specialist at the South End Health Center. Mary's large and gifted family have various and sundry challenging, interesting professions in metropolitan Boston. That evening, they graciously responded to Marie, who stayed for the entire party. Walter Senior stood for a long while, appearing ready to leave on a moment's notice. He finally sat down. Ernie Brown, my sister's husband, befriended him. They stayed on the comfortable couch, blending in with the many guests. No friend or relative made a comment about Walter's parents.

The wedding that followed was at St. Matthew's Episcopal Church in Worcester, with all the pomp and ceremony befitting the occasion. I do not recall if the married Reis children came from Colorado and Connecticut, but young Yvonne and her parents were there. Yvonne was fully involved in the event.

I did not dislike Marie. I took the position of pitying her rather than censuring. She continued to treat me as an exotic: a creature never before encountered. A year or more passed before Marie and I had an honest, serious conversation. She was profusely apologetic. I let her know I had never been confused by her apparent ignorance. I was well practiced at being civil to folks who had a lot to learn about people of color. She was not a complicated woman. Her husband and children came to know and love my daughter as much as Walter

Junior did. What brought Marie and me to the brink of friendship was the birth of the first grandchild, Ariane Alexis. Hearts melted and mingled. Conversations and sharing became routine. Marie became Mimi, and I became Granma. This grandchild was the first on both sides of the family. It was some years later that Marie's other married children began families.

Marie and I became life-long friends. When her husband died, my daughters and granddaughter were deeply saddened. He adored Ariane. We met at family affairs and in airports and, in the spring of 2011, we gathered in Austin for our shared granddaughter's wedding. By phone, Marie and I planned a group wedding gift of a honeymoon stay at a hotel the couple longed to visit: the St. Cecilia. It is pricey and funky and right in the newlyweds' neighborhood.

Marie's health was failing, and Ariane made sure a wheelchair was available so Mimi could keep up with all the pre- and post-wedding activities. I was using a walker: just months before the wedding, I had dislocated and fractured my ankle when hit by a car while crossing the street. Marie and I laughed at the thought of our both wheeling around at the reception. We were not going to miss the occasion, no matter what. She traveled from Florida, and I flew in from Massachusetts. Our connection was sweet, full of happy times and, of course, Marie's retelling of how we met.

Marie was a talented storyteller and had no qualms about laughing at her shortcomings. She never tired of telling our story: the circumstances, her racism, her epiphany and our growing friendship. That Irish heritage sparkled when she retold the same story with

113

embellishments and asides guaranteed to provoke laughter. No matter how long or complex the joke, she recalled it, timed it to perfection and dropped in the punch line like a professional comedian. I knew that without Walter Senior by her side, there was pain beneath her merriment on this day. Perhaps this talent always helped her cope with life's cruelties.

That August, she was retelling the story of our first encounter at another family gathering. We were together again: both families. The bride's father, Marie's gentle son, my first son-in-law, the nurse who had gone to university with my daughter after his years as a medic in the Air Force, had died instantly in a motorcycle accident in Genesee, Colorado on Tuesday, August 30, 2011.

Marie & Walter Reis

We were at his brother Michael's home in Denver. Marie was talking a great deal, even joking. When I asked how she was doing, she admitted, "Shirley, I'm still numb. Like this isn't real." I had a similar feeling. We talked about the wakes and funerals we were familiar with from our youth: the casket in the parlor, the calling hours, and the open and closed casket events.

I said, "There's something unnerving about a photograph and a small black box with an orchid lying on it." She stared at me and asked, "Was that Walter...in that box?" She had wondered and not dared to ask. There was such ceremony, so many people, so many tributes, uniforms, twenty-one-gun salute, "Taps." We stayed outside on the deck together until darkness fell. The house was still full of family, friends and neighbors. It was real.

CHAPTER 22

The Ceremony

The Veterans Administration arranged the entire ceremony. It was held in the lower-level auditorium of the VA Hospital where Walter worked. He was assigned to the intensive care unit and had been a member of the team for over twenty years.

A gallery of large photographs of Walter ran along the walkway to the auditorium. Some were serene portraits, others included family members and workmates; inside the auditorium were Air Force photos and memorabilia. Before people were seated, co-workers guided people to sign the guest book and then invited each person to write a message to the family. Pads of paper and pens were available in the foyer. They planned to put the messages together and give the collection to the family. I picked up a pen and found my mind blank. I wrote nothing.

Family filled every seat in the front rows. When the hall hushed, I turned and saw a standing room only crowd: immediate family, extended family, former patients, neighbors and friends. Many who stood were workmates and hospital administrators.

The low platform in front held a spray of flowers and greenery. The chaplain mounted the stage and led prayers and hymns. He then invited family and friends to speak. Marie's youngest daughter, Yvonne, gave an honest delight-filled eulogy. Laughter was inevitable as we who knew Walter recognized his quirky stubbornness and good heart. The widow, his second wife, gave a dynamic tribute with such deliberate calm that it was uncanny. She spoke as if from a speaker's bureau, confident of winning the prize. I only knew her as a restrained, aloof person who resisted all overtures made to befriend her. I could not resist complimenting her and admitting I had failed to really know her because of the years she held her distance from her husband's first wife and extended family. She confirmed her aloof posture, explaining, "I didn't want to intrude." She remained smiling, radiant and composed the remainder of the day. It was chilling. Walter's only child and her husband sat beside the widow. Ari and Mark's wedding, just months previous, had been a joyous occasion for all of the folks in the front rows.

Neighbors spoke, sharing more stories. One marveled at how Walter adored his daughter and went to the library to get books about how to braid hair. A former patient told a tender story of how Walter badgered her to reclaim her sight and mobility. When she told him she just wanted to jump out a window and end it all, Walter admonished her and joked, "OK, but not on my shift!" She proudly let us all see that she had indeed regained her sight and her mobility as a result of Walter's tough love.

The spontaneous eulogies brought both laughter and tears. The service ended with a solo by a VA Hospital employee: A song by Josh Groban, expertly delivered. The family rose, and participants came forward to greet us. I wandered about the hall, thanked the soloist and sought out the former patient. There were light refreshments, and all were invited to attend the burial at the National Cemetery in Denver.

There was a small window of time to grab lunch. Our family group of five included me, Mia and her second husband, Brian, and their son Liam, and Ari and Mark. We ate lightly, taking home half of our food to finish at the hotel. We had directions to the cemetery and were glad we arrived early. It was a city of crosses. Mesmerizing. The geometric, exacting rows spread endlessly across what seemed like miles. A cemetery crew in a golf cart led us to the correct section.

The Air Force honor squad did themselves proud: flag folding, a twenty-one-gun salute and a skilled bugler's rendition of "Taps." Walter's portrait and the small black box with orchid on top rested on a table with a spray of roses. Veterans lined one side of the path, saluting as we entered. On the left, a contingent of bikers lined up on the roadside. I asked, "Did Walter belong to a motorcycle group?" A knowledgeable voice answered, "No, these men and women attend the funerals of all bikers who die on our roads." Who knew? The sun shone brightly, the breeze was gentle, the ceremony spectacular. It was over, and I felt privileged to be there to say goodbye to Marie's gentle son, Walter Joseph Reis, Jr.

CHAPTER 23

Saying Goodbyes

Death is more universal than life; everyone dies but not everyone lives.

—Alan Sachs

Not long ago, I spent an evening with a group of wonderful people who gathered to contemplate the best ways to say goodbye to a treasured leader and friend. Dottie Curry was seeking care and comfort in her last days of life.

Before one of the members of this gathering suggested our getting together, I had already spent time thinking about the growing numbers of goodbyes I have experienced, and the ones I expect will soon be upon me. It's autumn for me: a time of color, coolness, the onset of death in preparation for fertilization and regeneration.

My earliest memory of death was Jocko, our mixed Spitz dog. We figured he had been poisoned as his bodily functions suddenly went into violent expulsions. We held him, cleaned him and tried soothing his agony with reassuring words. We buried him in the backyard, and a small fir tree spontaneously grew right on his grave.

Perhaps the death of a pet and the manner in which

adults explain it creates a child's lasting feelings about this special kind of goodbye.

I was five when my grandfather died. He lived next door. I loved him deeply and assisted him at his job of janitor at my school. Whenever he went to the market, you could watch for him coming up the path to his house and know for sure – he had a treat for you. The best one was the sweet drop cookie with a raisin on top.

I do not remember tears at his funeral. I was naturally sad and felt he might have been frightened. He had left us so quickly and had to go alone. At the funeral parlor, I asked if I could write him a note. It was the funeral director who got the paper and pen and wrote down my message: "Don't be afraid, Gran'pa. I love you, Shirley." I was lifted up and was able to slip my note into his inside jacket pocket. He was wearing a nice brown suit.

One classmate died while I was in grammar school. She was a brave, beautiful girl with golden curls and gentle blue eyes. Her bravery had to do with her willingness to invite the only two Colored girls in the school to enter the girls' recess games. It did not worry her what others thought, and she was so admired by all that they dared not ridicule her or call her names, like nigger lover.

Before the sixth grade, Betty developed childhood leukemia and was unable to return to school after her treatments. The teachers informed us that she was never going to return to school. I was devastated and wanted to say goodbye. My sister and I went to her house and knocked on the door. Her mother gently informed us that Betty could not have visitors. She was too ill. We made it clear that we would not disturb her.

We simply wanted to say goodbye. Betty recognized our voices and bid her mother to let us in. We were beckoned to the window where we could see each other. We spoke to her and noticed her bald head and the many lumps that covered her face. Her eyes were still blue and gentle. We smiled at each other and did not need many words.

We went to the funeral parlor. The casket was closed. My sister remembers the name of the funeral parlor. I just remember feeling privileged that we were the only classmates who got to visit her.

In high school, we lost a classmate who drowned as her non-swimming parents watched. Her name was Natasha Korobokoff, and her empty chair haunted us. I thought mostly about her immigrant parents and how tragic her death had been.

Sickness and the care of the sick became my career at the age of seventeen. I entered nursing school, and that first year an upperclassman died. All students were given time to go to Maria's wake. It was sobering, and I was not prepared for what I saw: Maria Quintiliani in the coffin in a pure white lace bridal gown! Her folded hands held rosary beads, and she had a beautiful gold ring on her finger. I was struck dumb and then frantically sought explanations: what did she die of? The answer was lupus erythematosus. I had never heard of it and, until she died, it seems the doctors were not sure what made her so ill. Why was she in a bridal gown? The answer: her family was old fashioned Italian, and since she was a virgin she was married to God at her death. Dear Lord, I prayed that I would never have lupus erythematosus. The vision of Maria in her coffin never left me. I have since learned many people have lupus and survive.

With the years, understanding has come. Even the freshest, most beautiful flowers die, as do some children. The older folks who die understand they must at some time let go of life. They have made some peace or conjured some dread, but they know the time will come. One of my mother's workmates, Harry Gaumond, grew weary of writing Christmas cards and asked my mother to write them for him. He apologized each year, saying, "I didn't think I'd be here another year. Do you mind doing my cards one more time?"

I have to be truthful: I do not like saying goodbye. So please stick around as long as you can, and I'll do likewise.

Index of Photographs

Introduction
Author in Uniform viii
Thirsty: My Journey to Drink It All In
Early 12 Ellen Street #1 5
Herbert and Dorothy's Daughters
Dorothy at early 12 Ellen Street 13
Audrey and Shirley in the Snow circa 1934 17
Looking Like Topsie
Shirley circa 1937 20
Ten-Yard Roller
Shirley & Audrey 1952 42
Love Letters
First Page of Oscar's 1987 Letter 47
Oscar D. Carter 1987 48
Sparrow
Flight School. Shirley in the Cockpit of Cessna 54
Stellar Events
The Olympic Torch Passing the Flame 59
The Sisterhood
Bassett Lane Cabins 78
Eliane Remax Nagle Landry Harrison
Eliane and Shirley 85
Daytona Beach
Eliane on Motorcycle 89
Jogging, Junkets & Just Plain Fun
Inés & Shirley on Tandem Bicycle 97
Deep Water Harbor
Our Mothers: Rebecca & Dorothy 106
Saying Goodbye
Marie & Walter Reis 114

CPSIA information can be obtained
at www.ICGtesting.com
Printed in the USA
BVHW042316080621
609012BV00003BA/520